JESSICA HUGHES AND CONTRIBUTORS

The Creative Lifebook

Reflections On The Art Of Living A Fully Expressed Life

ILLUMINATED PRESS
·BOOK PUBLISHING·

First edition

ISBN: 9798392006885

Cover art by Jessica Hughes
Advisor: Kamila Behrens

This book was professionally typeset on Reedsy.
Find out more at reedsy.com

Contents

Foreword

By Dr. Joe Vitale

Try something with me.

Open this book anywhere.

Go ahead. Do it right now.

What did you find?

Do it again. Open the book anywhere.

What did you find this time?

Pretty cool, right?

You can open this book anywhere, at any time, no matter who you are or what you do, and you will find a useful tip—a shortcut, a hack, an insight, a method, a tool—to help unlock and unblock your creative juices.

And believe me, we all need this.

As humans, we are all innately creative. Yes, even you. However, with the hustle and bustle of everyday life, with all the distractions we have on a moment-by-moment basis, it's easy to get stuck in a rut and feel like we've lost touch with our creative side.

We've all been there. I may have written 80 books and recorded 15 albums, but I still seek out new ways to open myself to the creative flow. I regard it as my mystical quest. It's me looking for spirituality through creative expression.

That's where this book comes in—it's a collection of creativity techniques that anyone can use within minutes to spark their imagination, think outside the box, and tap into their inner artist.

Whether you're an artist, writer, designer, sculptor, cartoonist, or just someone looking to infuse a little more creativity into your daily routine, this book has something for you. The techniques included are easy to follow and will help you break free from creative blocks, unleash your imagination, and bring your ideas to life.

It will help bring fire and light to whatever you are doing or long to do. It will heal you, help you, and reconnect you to the most powerful source of all: creativity. The practical ideas in this unique book are from wellness experts, therapists, fertility experts, women's health authorities, authors, artists, mothers, and more. In other words, real people practicing real creativity.

You're in for a treat. From brainstorming exercises to visualization techniques, this book is designed to get your creative juices flowing and help you tap into your fullest potential. You'll learn how to silence your inner critic, generate new ideas, and turn your wildest dreams into reality. You'll also discover insights that just plain surprise and delight you.

So, if you're ready to unleash your creativity and explore your full potential, then this book is for you. It's time to let your imagination run wild and see what amazing things you can create.

Hmmm. I wonder what you will create next.

Flip open the book and let's see...

Expect Miracles!

Dr. Joe Vitale

Author, Speaker, Musician, Inspirator

Host, Zero Limits Living e-TV

www.MrFire.com

Preface

YOU were made to run wild.

To create.

To EXPERIENCE the magic of expressing your own unique stamp in the world.

This book is the starting point to spark your creativity so you can reignite JOY and experience greater well-being and fulfillment in your life. We're here to reawaken that child within you that's tired of adulting. Who may even be hungry for another way to explore meaning or express the emotion that may be churning inside. Who is ready to bring their FULL self to the table of life.

If you believe you "aren't creative," this book is for you.

Because Creating is for everyone.

The concept for this book was not something I planned in advance. I am passionate about spotlighting and amplifying the voices of creatives, but I never anticipated the scope of a project like this.

The collective vision was a divinely gifted "download" that whooshed through my system and came through me with so much electricity and power that I HAD to act on it.

Part of that vision was for the content to be sourced from MANY creative minds, not just mine. Nearly 70 of us gathered to collaborate and create something from nothing. To give YOU the gift of our best and most potent creative ideas.

Knowing that the world is only speeding up with content overload—I wanted to gift a book to you that was valuable, brief, and easy to consume in small windows of time.

I want this to be a book that is thumbed through, bookmarked, dog-eared, and doodled upon. I want you to use this as a transformational framework to experience more play and joy in your life.

This is also an EASY book that can be explored ANY way you'd like.

Read it from the end to the beginning. Flip it open anywhere. Read only what nudges you, excites you, and especially the ideas that scare you. Stretch outside your comfort zone and just begin with something that resonates with you. An idea that sparks a bit of hummingbird energy within, or boosts your smile a smidge. Trust yourself to know where to begin. You have brilliance inside. Your soul is beckoning you forward to play in the realm of joy and magic.

It's no accident that you're here.

We have 65 artists, thought leaders, wellness experts, coaches, and intuitives who have all contributed their favorite SINGLE idea to help you bring greater creativity into your world.

We are a collective of heart led entrepreneurs leading people to experience the incredible growth and expansion that occurs when you connect to your intuition, to your creative genius, to your playful self.

And when you're ready for more, we've created a whole directory online at www.creativelifebook.com to share additional videos, training, and super fun exercises you can dig into to take your favorite ideas one step further.

Being an artist is the secret key behind running an uber successful online business. I paint because it makes me better at business. I paint to stay clean and sober. I paint to have a place to express the non-verbal when words are too limited for the gamut of emotion I experience in this delicious human experience.

I paint to fill my cup to overflowing, and when my light is overflowing, everyone around me benefits.

This book wouldn't exist if I didn't claim my right to play in the realm of creative magic.

Now it's your turn. Carve out some time to daydream, to play, to fill your own cup in a world far away from technology.

And when you're ready for more, come find us.

To the embers that flow inside you that are ready to be sparked into a wildfire...I'm cheering you on!

Jessica Hughes

I

Phase 1: UnBlock & ReAwaken

Feeling creatively blocked can be frustrating and discouraging, but the following experts are here to help reawaken your inner creative! By tackling the root cause and embracing activities that promote self-expression and relaxation (without judgment), the creative juices can start flowing again. So let's ditch the funk and ignite that spark of inspiration for a happier and more fulfilling life!

1

Boredom: The Direct Portal to Creativity by Jessica Hughes

G et Bored. On purpose.

Say, what?

Most of us are so USED to racing around like chickens with their heads cutoff. Exhausted, anyone?

From over scheduled kids, to overworked and underpaid, the exhaustion and burnout can be very real.

The world is FAST pace, and it's just picking up speed. Everyone seems to be racing towards some unspoken destination that we can't articulate—we just know that we're LATE. And we don't want to be left behind.

Not enough time, not enough money, not enough hours in the day. Scarcity rules the minds. It can leave people unfulfilled and worn down, like all this caring for others will never end. Has anyone ever told you to intentionally get bored? Probably not. It's counter to all the books on productivity, smart goals, success and hustling. What if I told you it is the DIRECT portal to the juiciest creativity of all?

A serious pattern disrupt.

It's a big ZIG, when the whole world is zagging.

Try it. I promise that untold magic awaits you. Boredom has been the key to my own transformation and accelerated success, (but that's a story for another book.)

Boredom is the fuel that drives your creativity.

You may be thinking, "But, how do we "get bored" when life is packed to the gills?"

I've got you, friend!

The steps to PREPARE for boredom are outlined below. Get ready to disrupt the norm!

1. UN-EVERYTHING: First, identify the dead weight: Take a good, hard look at your life, your social media feeds (even email) and identify the people, brands, and content that are bringing you down or simply taking up space. These are the ones that gotta go. You're leaking energy by letting all that negativity and distraction in. Next, unfollow, unsubscribe, and unfriend with wild abandon. Then take a huge sigh of relief. Only the hell-yes remains.

2. BOUNDARIES: JUST SAY NO. First, identify your priorities. Figure out what truly matters to you and what gets you fired up. These are the things you want to protect and prioritize (like your life depends on it!) Then practice saying no to absolutely everything. Have the courage to put yourself first (hint: this won't feel comfortable!) Then, say no to anything that doesn't align with your priorities or make you feel

excited and energized. Keep saying no until you can tune into your own intuition, when you can hear and feel, your body knows what the "hell-yes" things really are. THEN, stick to your boundaries. This is where the rubber meets the road, my friend. Stick to your boundaries like your creativity depends on it (hint: it does!). Be firm, be consistent, and don't back down.

3. CREATE WHITESPACE: Make room for nothing. Schedule some down-time in your day with no set plans or expectations. Cancel everything that isn't mandatory. Create SPACE in your life. Let yourself wander aimlessly, doodle mindlessly, or simply stare at the ceiling and let your mind wander.

4. DITCH THE SCREENS: Shut down your computer, silence your phone, and unplug from the digital world. Let your brain breathe and roam free from the constant buzz of notifications and distractions. (Hint: Boredom while watching TikTok isn't real boredom.)

5. ZEN OUT: Carve out some time to meditate, reflect, or simply sit in silence. Let your thoughts and ideas percolate without judgment or interruption. Invite curiosity into your mind and simply observe the thoughts you think. Then go to bed early for a week. Get too MUCH rest, then watch what happens. Boredom isn't just a mind-numbing snooze-fest—it's actually the secret sauce to unlocking your creative potential. When you're bored, your mind is free to wander, explore, and take risks. You're not tied down by obligations or distractions, which means you can really tune into your own thoughts and feelings. And that's where the magic happens!

This creativity hack is the one that connects you directly to the portal of your inner creativity. ALL that follows in the rest of the book will allow you to dive deep into everything that awaits you.

Remember, no one will make all this space FOR you, so you must do it for yourself...and create the relief that invites creativity like a magnet.

*Jessica Hughes is a visibility expert for creative entrepreneurs as well as an internationally collected fine artist, #1 bestselling author, and mom of seven. She is founder of **Jess Hughes Media** and **Illuminated Press**, a boutique publishing company created to amplify the voices of thought leaders, artists, creatives, educators, and experts.*

*She is the visionary behind **The Creative Lifebook**. Her passion is supporting the audience growth of hidden gem entrepreneurs so they can step into the spotlight, lead with confidence, and illuminate our world. She offers educational programs, courses, and coaching to support value driven leaders with their mission to create true impact in the world. She teaches the mindset, skillset, and inspired action to be unstoppable.*

Hughes has been a featured expert on ABC, NBC, FOX, TED, Forbes, Chopra, and more.

* * *

2

The Cycle of Your Creative Flow by Annette Mariel

D id you know that syncing your menstrual cycle to your life can be a game-changer not only to your health but your creative flow?

It's true! Our cycles follow four phases—menstrual, follicular, ovulatory, and luteal—and each one comes with its own unique strengths and challenges. This is due to the hormones that shift throughout the month.

I'm sure if you are a female, you have felt your own creative shifts throughout the month. Some weeks you are in an effortless creative flow but then it could feel like a shift out of nowhere, you feel like someone turned off your creative faucet. By understanding your unique rhythms and strengths, you can tailor your creative pursuits to make the most of every phase of your cycle. So go ahead and embrace your cycle—your creativity will thank you for it!

Let's start understanding your monthly creative flow:

During your menstrual phase, it's all about taking some time to slow down and reflect. You might feel a little more introspective and less energetic, but that doesn't mean you can't tap into your creative flow. Take some time to journal, meditate, or just curl up with a good book. You never know what insights you might gain that will fuel your creativity later!

As your body moves out of the slower, more introspective phase of menstruation and into the follicular and ovulatory phases, you will experience a surge in energy, motivation, and optimism if you are honoring each phase. If you do not properly rest during menstrual you can run the risk of stealing the power from the follicular. Each phase has its powers and the more we optimize them the more creative flow we will have.

The follicular and ovulatory phases are when women typically experience a surge in creativity, energy, and inspiration. This is the perfect time to start new projects, take on creative challenges, and experiment with new ideas. You may find that your mind is buzzing with new inspiration and you're more open to trying new things.

The follicular phase specifically is associated with a sense of renewal and fresh starts, making it an ideal time for creative pursuits.

Don't be afraid to take risks and try something new—this is your time to shine!

As you move into your ovulatory phase, you're feeling social and outgoing. This typically occurs around day 14 of a 28-day cycle, when estrogen levels are at their peak. This hormonal surge can lead to increased confidence, assertiveness, and a sense of purpose. This is the perfect time to collaborate with other creatives, seek out new inspiration, and bounce ideas off your friends. Who knows—you might even come up with your next big idea during a brainstorming session with your favorite people.

In addition to these hormonal shifts, the increased energy and confidence that come with the follicular and ovulatory phases can also be attributed to a psychological phenomenon known as the "pink cloud effect." This refers to a period of elevated mood and motivation.

The follicular and ovulatory phases are ideal times for creative pursuits. Whether you're a writer, artist, musician, or any other type of creative, harnessing the energy and inspiration of these phases can help you tap into your inner creative goddess.

Finally, during your luteal phase, things might start to feel a little more challenging. You might be dealing with mood swings and fatigue, which can make it tough to stay focused and productive. But don't worry—with a little extra self-care and mindfulness, you can still tap into your creative flow. Take breaks when you need them, practice some gentle yoga, and give yourself permission to slow down and take care of yourself.

By understanding your unique rhythms and strengths, you can tailor your creative pursuits to make the most of every phase of your cycle.

By embracing your cycle—you will tap into your creative genius effortlessly!

I'm Annette Mariel, certified holistic nutrition consultant, hormone balance specialist and founder of Sexy Hormones. My goal is to demystify the science of female hormones so you can live a radiant and SEXY life. Having suffered and

successfully reversed my own PCOS, hypothyroidism, chronic bloating, fatigue, weight gain and PMS—I know all the unsuspecting ways hormonal imbalances manifest in the body.

Through cycle tracking, nutrition education, hormone-friendly exercise, and the removal of external toxins I was able to successfully balance my own hormones, heal my symptoms AND help others do the same!

My teachings help empower women with the science, root causes and action steps needed to achieve optimal hormonal balance—AKA the happiest, healthiest, sexiest and most creative version of YOU!

https://www.instagram.com/iamannettemariel/?hl=en

* * *

3

Rest is the Best Tool in Your Productivity Toolbox by Cami Baker Miller

I t took a cancer diagnosis and a subsequent year of treatment for me to truly learn the value of rest. Every once in a while, I need to be reminded just how far I've come. Before cancer, I was go! go! go! Keep doing, keep pushing, keep improving. I remember one time I got sick enough to leave work early. I ended up lying on the couch IN THE LIGHT OF DAY and thinking how novel and strange it felt.

Learning to be still, say no, play more, and protect my free time are just a few of the awesome lessons cancer and treatment brought me. I fiercely protect my free time and my alone time now.

It's hard to always keep this in perspective. It was a hard-won lesson, but when most of the people you surround yourself with are still productivity and activity driven, it's sometimes hard NOT to feel lazy. To wonder what they must be thinking when you say no to a request.

The time since my diagnosis has been a study in remembering that balance between work and playtime, and how to stay at home in my own body, soul, and mind. To stay quiet, calm, and still.

To remember that sometimes rest is the most productive activity you can practice in the moment.

Learning is a spiral. I can look back and see the progress I made since the last time this came up. I can remember what worked last time, what didn't work so well, and adjust accordingly.

Rest and play do NOT have to be earned. They are your BIRTHRIGHT. They lead to bigger, better, bolder ideas. They lead to renewed energy and enthusiasm. They lead to growth.

Rest is what ultimately led me back to the canvas, and it, coupled with play, also help me navigate blocks and help get me back in the creative genius zone when my inspiration and energy are floundering.

I like to think I have gotten very VERY good at rest. You could even say I have taken it to new levels of achievement... I've spent full work days lying in bed just watching movies, napping, reading something for pure pleasure—and felt absolutely no remorse for it. I suggest making rest a part of your day long before you get stuck or blocked. Rest leads to renewal—in body, soul, heart, mind. And Rest + Play + Renewal = new energetic pathways being created. And you know what that leads to—yep... more creativity, productivity and ease.

Ways to incorporate rest into your daily life:

1. Nap Time! Anything from 15 minutes to all damn day. You do you.
2. Meditation—you're ultimately learning to still and quiet your mind, allowing for all kinds of new inspiration to flood in.
3. Read a book for pure pleasure.
4. Pile up in bed with a favorite movie.
5. Remember—moving your body is still resting your mind. Get outside and take a walk in nature, put on your favorite music and dance around,

do some yoga—again, you do you, boo!

6. I would include any hobby you love doing—again, getting out of your mind and into your body is still considered rest in my book.

7. While I would agree that any small amount of rest is more beneficial than not taking that pause, my favorite thing to do is to play hooky ALL DAY LONG! I will do NOTHING I do not want to do that day. I put my phone on DND, and become a hermit for the day.

8. Hug a tree—for at least 3 minutes. Really—get out there and wrap your arms around a tree, heart to bark. Your heart rate will slow, your breathing will even out... no, this is not a scientific study—just something I've experienced. I promise, your whole body will thank you.

This is by no means an exhaustive list. Some of these may make you cringe and think "I can't do THAT!" This is when I ask you to remember that it's a practice—something you do imperfectly and improve on over time. Some things may resonate, some can be tweaked, and there may be some you think of that feel like rest to you. We are all different beautiful people and the variety of our personalities and desires are what make this crazy world so special.

Cami Baker Miller is an abstract artist, writer, cancer thriver, and mindset coach. She found her way to NLP and coaching via her art thanks to a cancer diagnosis

in late 2018. Since then, it has been her mission to help women clear their head trash and get consistent in their creativity so they can live their best life.

https://beacons.ai/camibakermiller

* * *

4

How to Gain Access to Your Creative Energy One Day at a Time by Jenny Manno

Each morning I give myself the time to empower my manifesting and intuition practices by engaging in my 55 x 5 manifesting affirmations and Tarot/Oracle readings.

55 x 5 is a law of attraction technique that requires you to write manifestation affirmations 55 times per day for 5 days. This process creates alignment in your subconscious, causing it to believe your biggest desires are already true.

Below I will share with you two very attainable ways to get the best possible benefits and use out of your valuable time and affirmation/intuition practices.

Below is a guide on how to implement these practices for the "no time to spare days."

For the "I have all the time in the world, days" visit my website for a more in depth training.

Why is the practice of 55 x 5 manifestation/affirmation and Tarot/Oracle readings so important?

We live very busy, very full lives and feel more disconnected than ever to ourselves and those around us and we ache for connection, love, friendship, inspiration and trust. Wouldn't it be amazing to without a shadow of a doubt TRUST your very own intuition? No questions asked! Wouldn't it be incredible to find that deep, real love and friendship for yourself maybe even for the first time? The problem is we just stopped listening. These practices will give you the guidance and tools to actually HEAR via your intuition what you already know and trust it implicitly, as well as allow you to connect to your higher vibrational energy which will ignite your manifestation affirmations and turn them into reality!

How to commit to your manifestation/affirmation practice on the days that time is short:

1. Grab a lined journal and number it from 1- 55. (every affirmation you will do 5 days in a row and then repeat with a new affirmation)
2. At the top of the page write out your affirmation/manifestation completely. Example: I am right now living in my highest vibrational timeline! Then from 1 to 55 write it out as an INITIALISM (it's an abbreviation that uses the first letter of each word in the phrase) Not all initialisms are acronyms.
3. As you write the letters: IARNLIMHVT you repeat the words in your head (not the initials) 55 times.

You can do more, I often do to really rev up my manifesting energy. Have a smile on your face as you do it. You can even sing the words in your head as you write them. HAVE FUN WITH IT! It's all about the EMOTION you are feeling as you write. THAT is what turns up your vibrational energy! Your desires/manifestations are already waiting for you... all they need is YOUR excitement to be able to find you!

How to gain access to your creative energy by using a Tarot/Oracle Deck when you don't have a lot of time to spare:

Start with the 4 x 4 mindful breathing exercise. Close your eyes and breathe in through your nose to a count of 4, then hold it for 4, then release it to a count of 4 and hold it again for a count of 4. I like to picture myself creating a box one line at a time with each 4 count that floats just outside of my solar plexus Chakra (which represents personal strength, learning and comprehension).

The benefits of mindful breathing before a reading are to help you quiet the mind so that you can hear how your intuition is trying to guide you by releasing endorphins from the brain to promote a sense of relaxation and calm.

When you are ready to pull your cards ALWAYS start with "For my highest good" I ask my Angels and Guides to use my intuition to _____ and fill in the blank. Example: "For my highest good, I ask my Angels and Guides to use my intuition to show me what it is I need to do/see/hear in order to fulfill the vision I have for my creative life?"

Using your favorite deck, with your eyes closed repeat the question and shuffle your cards. If you are short on time, I suggest pulling only one card after asking your question and displaying it somewhere you will see it often for the remainder of the day so that you can sit with the message that your intuition is trying to tell you. In your deck there will be a guidebook on several different options on how to lay out your cards for a reading. (This is up to you and can change from day to day.) Remember, there are no black and white answers but with continued practice you will start to notice patterns and a certain language/connection that your guides and Angels use when connecting with you through your intuition/thoughts.

Now that you've written out your 55 affirmations and pulled your cards… get ready, because this is where there are no rules and you can let creativity decide what's next!

Artist, Teacher, Creativepenuer https://www.jennymanno.com/ To learn more about me and how to 'Gain access to your creative energy one day at a time' visit my website for a more in depth demonstration on how to use the "Magic of 55 x 5 and Tarot/Oracle readings!" It's time to level-up and activate your highest creative self!

https://www.jennymanno.com/

* * *

5

Using The Wild to Reset and Recover by Jodi Kincaid

When life feels overwhelming or like my head might explode and my creative self is at a loss—my soul craves the wild. I truly believe our souls need wild spaces to reset and recover. To center and ground ourselves. To see that there is something bigger happening around us.

The wild allows our souls to rest. The quiet sounds of nature hum with promise and peace. The ebb and flow of the tides, the wild and untamed sea, and the thick gushing of rivers moving downstream can be a conduit for peace. If we allow time and space in nature our physical bodies and crowded minds can settle and feel the wonder of the wild. Each tiny shell or river rock has had a journey all its own. The soft ferns and tangled roots tell a story of a life of triumph over the elements. There is both history and hope in natural places. If we take a few moments to actually stop and observe nature the Divine has a way of settling our souls.

The organic order of nature can fuel creativity. It has the perfect composition. The hard and soft edges of stones, beautiful twisted roots and branches of trees, water both opaque and transparent. If we allow ourselves to be saturated in the wonder of it all the wild can transform our hearts and smooth our rough edges. The same way the flow of the river smooths the sharp edges of a rock or how the tossing of the sea can polish a shell and smooth out rough branches into soft driftwood.

There are whole ecosystems in tide pools and puddles or at the bases of trees. Nature has a way of turning hard places soft and creating beauty from destruction and degradation. Mushrooms flourish on decaying trees, barnacles attach to abandoned shells to survive. Some of the most beautiful elements in nature are the ones that have been worn down by time. We would never see the beautiful veins of color running through stones if they had not been broken or worn down by the water continually running over them and wearing away at them. Treasured sea glass is a result of jagged edges being tossed over and over against the sand until they are smooth and rounded. Tiny flowers push their way through the most compacted unforgiving areas to bloom.

When we are feeling jagged and depleted, wild places can feed our soul and creativity if we will allow ourselves to just stop and breathe. If we take a moment to actually feel with our body and spirit we can become more settled, more organized, more a part of the whole instead of separated, harried and alone. Our souls need the wild. Nature is a gift to us—we only have to receive it. The stars, moon, ebb & flow of the tide, intricate patterns of flowers, and the soft sweet flow of the river. All of these things and so much more are here for us as tools, talismans, comforters and encouragers to our souls.

Which in turn causes our creativity to bloom and flourish.

We just need to take a few minutes...

Jodi Kincaid is a heart-centered intuitive artist, and grounded idealist. She believes our souls need the wild—to reclaim hope, foster peace, and connect to the Divine. Her art is collected in both the US and internationally.

http://jodikincaidprints.com/

https://www.jodikincaid.com/

* * *

6

Embark on a Hobby-Seeking-Journey by Gabriela Ortiz

H i, my name is Gabriela Ortiz and I help those that feel stuck in any area of their lives get inspired everyday through art and creative tools.

Before starting my creative journey, I was totally blocked. I had the belief that I was not creative and that you were either born with creativity or you weren't. I took pride in being a numbers and process oriented person; but to be frank, I felt burned out at work and knew something was missing from my life.

I used to think that museums were boring, because I went to one when I was eight years old. As an adult, I vacationed in Madrid and visited the Prado Museum. I was surprised by how much I enjoyed the visit. I felt like a child looking at all the art, mesmerized by the subjects, the brushstrokes and colors. My heart felt happy, like I was in love for the first time. But when I went back home, I went back to my old routine, quickly forgot about the magic of the museum and felt the burnout again.

This time, I decided to go on a hobby-seeking journey. I was determined to get unstuck. I enrolled in every class available that piqued my interest. During an eighteen month period, I took belly dancing, violin, singing, painting, yoga, and golf lessons. I even joined a singing choir!

I didn't judge whether I was any good at any of these activities (hint, I wasn't). I just leaned into the experience and asked myself: Do I look forward to it? Does it feel good? What is the part of it that I enjoy? Am I having fun? For some of us, a challenge feels good, while for others, relaxation is the goal. It all depends on our personality.

My advice for unleashing your creativity is to go on a hobby-seeking journey. It's like taking yourself on fun creative dates, and seeing what happens. You are not committing to anything yet, you are just experiencing the variety available. I recommend going on your own, whenever possible, to avoid being biased by others' preferences. Discovering what you like, brings joy and enriches your life. It helps you understand and voice your preferences. Trying something new makes us grow as a person and create better social connections. You will be surprised by what you learn about yourself and how this knowledge positively changes your life.

But where to start?

Start with curiosity: Is there something that's always interested you, but you've never tried? Or something you loved doing, but you've left behind?

Look for classes in close proximity to your home or if you prefer sign up on-line, and give it a go. Make it easy on yourself. Anything goes: a cooking class, knitting, fishing, drawing, scrapbooking, dancing, wood working, wine tasting. The list is endless. And above all, be patient with yourself. If you've neglected your creative side, this may feel a bit uncomfortable at first, and you may need to give it some time. Avoid judging or disqualifying yourself before trying something new. We are all new at something at some point and everything gets easier and better with time.

Finding a hobby that you are passionate about can change your life. I am happy to report that I found my passion at that museum. I enrolled in painting classes, and paint every chance I get. After 16 years of taking art classes, I quit my corporate job to become a full time artist and now get to enjoy my hobby every day. Best of all, I learned that my preconceived notions about who I was as a person were wrong. I am creative after all, and so are you!

Gabriela Ortiz is an artist and international best selling author, passionate about creating inspiring paintings to help people receive daily motivation to pursue their dreams.

As the founder of Gabriela Ortiz Art and Design, her mission is to help women that feel burnt out, improve their wellness, experience the healing power of art and awaken their creativity. (New paragraph)

You can find her artwork at https://www.gabrielaortizart.com

* * *

24

7

Quick Time Creating to Get in the Zone by Greta Olivas

I believe creativity plays a crucial role in our lives, as it allows us to engage in a form of play that is innate to human nature and fosters personal growth. Sadly, many individuals have been led away from creativity since childhood, when they were told that doing so is frivolous and unproductive.

Apart from the benefits of play, creativity also instills courage, inspires new ideas, and enhances our ability to understand the world around us. When we are wholly immersed in creative activities such as painting, we may feel a profound sense of connection to the divine, which can be described as being in the "zone."

It's not easy to turn off our thinking minds and get into a creative groove. But I will share some exercises that I use to help you get into that zone.

1. Start with 6 pieces of paper to paint on, maybe 5"x7" in size, and tape them down on a painting surface.
2. Pick about 5 colors of paint (I use acrylic paints), a few brushes and a

timer.

3. Think of an simple object you would like to paint (I like doing a vase with flowers or a pear, they are my easy go-to's).

4. I set my timer for 4 minutes (or sometimes 3) and start painting.

It's frantic, but it allows me to be fully present in the moment. No time to think, just pure creating. There are mistakes, drips, etc. but when it's done I realize that the things we think would be messed up are sometimes the best parts of the paintings! What I have learned from this exercise is to stop thinking and just do, that nothing is truly messed up, and sometimes the beauty is in the magic that happened without trying.

Now a lot of times some are not good at all, so I re-purpose those for more exercises.

I know it might sound a bit silly, but I honestly believe that if everyone tapped into their creative side and got in touch with their divine higher selves, the world would be so much better!

Greta Olivas' colorful paintings are filled with energy and emotions that reflect her understanding of the universe and our place within it. Her abstract style has the power to provoke emotions in viewers, and she considers it successful when

someone states they 'felt' the painting.

She has been creating art since she was a small child, but started painting professionally in 2001. Since she's mostly self-taught, she has also inspired other artists to start painting by teaching creativity workshops and also empowering them by teaching technical skills so they can get their work seen.

In the early 2000's Greta was involved with a local art guild where she quickly became Exhibit Co-Chair and eventually President of the guild. In 2011 she decided to focus on learning abstract techniques to find her own voice, where she found the style she paints in today, where she incorporates her personal growth as part of the energy of the paintings.

Greta's work is in collections internationally and she has been seen on the local news and has appeared on several podcasts over the years.

https://www.gretaolivas.com/

* * *

8

Charting a New Path by Wendy Meg Siegel

A t times in our lives, we may find ourselves at a crossroad, ready to create something new. Perhaps there has been a shift within ourselves or in our world, prompting us to forge a new path forward. But how do we begin to choose what we want to create next? Here is a process for taking stock of where you've been, in order to chart a course towards where you want to go. Whether you've recently retired, are facing a major life change, or simply want to pursue a new project or venture, this process may help you establish your next creative path. With some self reflection and brainstorming, you can take steps towards a project or goal that fills you up and brings you joy.

The Process: The goal is to open yourself up to what you might like to create in the months ahead. By allowing space for new thoughts and ideas to surface, you can make a fresh start with something you find fulfilling. Set aside some alone time in a comfortable space, conducive for self reflection. Gather your preferred writing tools. Write each of the following prompts on a separate sheet of paper, and generate your responses. You can tape them up around the room, on windows and walls, or spread them out on a table top for an easy brainstorming flow.

1. What are the creative projects and ideas I have already begun? (Include those that have been sitting on the back burner even if you don't have the motivation to complete them.)

2. What new projects, activities, and experiences have I wanted to pursue? What have I wanted to learn?

3. What are my hopes and dreams? (Write them down even if they feel too big or unimaginable in this moment. *Especially* the ones that feel too big or unimaginable.)

4. What are my past achievements and successes? What am I most proud of?

5. What are my skills and abilities… big or small. Which ones would I most want to utilize in a new venture?

6. What are some positive statements and affirmations to fuel any new direction. (Be your own personal cheerleader.)

7. What can I let go of that no longer serves me? What is rooted in the past that does not support what I want to create in my life now? What old expectations would be best for me to release?

8. What inspires me? Who inspires me?

9. Add any additional prompts that come to mind to support you moving forward.

This doesn't have to be completed all at once. It is a process of finding your way forward. Highlight any of the items that resonate with you, tug at your heart, or call to you.

Once you feel complete, let the process percolate over time, and see what rises to the surface. Set some intentions for the first couple of action steps you can take now. Follow any internal nudges, keep an open mind, and allow the possibilities to take shape.

Wendy Meg Siegel is a mixed media artist who utilizes raw canvas to create structure, layers, and texture in her paintings. Her work is inspired by spiritual concepts and ancient wisdom, often evoking a sense of peace and healing in those who view it. Wendy's dedication to sharing her art and creative journey is an inspiration to others, encouraging them to explore their own relationship with creativity. In addition to her artwork, Wendy has also published two gratitude journals, "The Gratitude Habit" and "Parenting the Gratitude Habit." These journals offer a simple yet powerful tool for cultivating greater joy and happiness in everyday life.

https://www.wendymegsiegel.com

* * *

9

Start an Art Journal and Just Play by Lynn Mazzoleni

Longing for something new, I picked up a sketchbook and started painting the pages without concern. I knew there were rules or best practices, but I decided to just do something and expect nothing. It was a beautiful escape from feelings of obligation and perfectionism, which frequently pushed me to check emails or read serious things usually pertaining to my career. You see, somehow I had been convincing myself that every waking second had to be productive. Until then, my favorite act of rebellion was to watch a movie or binge watch Netflix.

When I picked up that sketchbook, I was longing for creativity because the world of striving for a really great career became a world of justifying and checking off more and more boxes on a never-ending to do list. The more efficient I was, the more I got asked to do. While people say you should just say no, it was never that simple.

So I began to wonder how could something that started off so promising become something that felt more like a cage? Not having an answer, I turned to my inner child who was probably about 16. And, I just decided to do whatever I wanted in a simple black book with empty white pages. Some people would call it a sketchbook, but I called it an escape, and now I look back at that first art journal in awe of what I did and how I felt. Something transformative happened during that time, and fortunately, I have a record of that and the (re)start of my art journey.

So, now that you're intrigued, you're probably wondering, what if I can't draw, what if I don't have any artistic skill, or what if I don't know what to make? My answer to all of these questions is why don't you just play with color, marks, and collaged papers? My backup answer is it really doesn't matter even if you make a big ol' mess... this is all about having fun and learning by doing. In a sense that is what creativity is all about... just doing what we feel like and learning from it. And, my hypothesis is that's why our full-time careers are not fun anymore, because most of them do not allow for creativity and failed attempts at doing something new. So, remember there are no rules, just a few suggestions.

My absolute favorite art escape is making monoprints with a gel plate. They're so simple and so inexpensive to make, that you can make tens to hundreds of prints for just about the same amount of money. Then with the abundance of printed papers, you can rip or cut pages into pieces however you like and adhere them into your art journal. Remember there are no actual rules! Then using any drawing medium—pens, pencils, markers, crayons, pastels (really any type of pastel you like)—you can add marks. And, if for some reason you don't like those marks add another piece of paper... one of your monoprints or something you've printed out from a computer or perhaps something you cut out from any other pre-existing book or magazine. And, if you're feeling really brave, add some paint directly to the page.

I filled my first art journal in a matter of just a few months. I adhered a few things that were done on loose paper, including a few old drawings that I'd kept or other things that I tried. I journaled in the book during the pandemic and then covered up the words with paint. I wrote little life stories, including a funny message from a deceased family pet who liked to chase deer. I collaged in a few things from my daughter's trash pile including her math homework. I explored a few drawing techniques by first collaging in pictures that I drew over with thin layers of paint. I made pages with fun inspirational messages and I made pages with various strange concepts, one of which included a map page of Roswell, NM because I wanted to remember a trip that we made there almost a decade earlier. My pages are all for me. They have been shared with my immediate family only, but they're not something that I would want to post on social media.

Although looking at art journal posts on social media can be fun, I would very strongly caution you to just do whatever you feel like doing without much consideration to what others are doing and definitely do not compare your work with others. This art journal is for you and you cannot really know what prior experience the other people who post their work have.

Lynn Mazzoleni is an emerging artist and chemistry professor obsessed with color and feminine expression. She learned to embrace her creativity to enhance her university work and bring a touch of science into her artwork. She co-hosts the Art Infused Life Podcast with empowering artist stories and lives in Michigan's Upper Peninsula near Lake Superior.

https://lynnmazzoleni.com/

https://CLB.lynnmazzoleni.com

* * *

10

Breathing for Creatives by Evelyn Applin

Have you ever gotten to that place where your creative genius seems to have taken a vacation? Gone, kaput, skedaddled? You might start to wonder if it's ever going to return, or worse even start doubting it was ever there? So when you find yourself in that place where the flow isn't flowing what can you do?

Well, here is a way to breathe new genius into your creative life.

Breathing is essential to life, and for many creators, creating is as essential as breathing. It is life. Therefore learning how to breathe into creative flow is an essential skill.

You may be familiar with square or belly breathing. This is a 4 step breathing method designed to slow the anxious and stressful aspects of our days. If you are unfamiliar it goes like this:

1. Seated or lying in a comfortable position, place your hand on your belly, 3 fingers below your navel. Breathe in deeply through your nose for a count of 4,
2. Hold that breath for a count of 4.

3. Slowly breathe out all of the breath through your mouth for a count of 4

4. Rest for a count of 4. Repeat.

This will slow down your anxious state of fight or flight and bring you back to center. Practice this calming exercise a few times to get used to it. (You can start with a shorter count if you find the timing too long and work up to longer, or you may start with a longer count, whichever is comfortable for you).

If you are still feeling stressed you can use the following exercise to release more of the resistance in your body:

1. Place your hands face up at your sides and your feet flat on the floor. Breathe in, and with this breath imagine you are breathing fresh energy into your body from the earth (floor)

2. Hold this fresh energy in your body feeling it flowing through your veins for the count of 4

3. Release the breath slowly for a count of 4 while imagining old energy (resistance/stress) flowing down your arms and disbursing out your fingertips

4. Rest for a count of 4. Repeat until you feel all of the resistance has dissipated.

When you are ready, I would like to invite you to take this breathing method a step further with some visualization and colour:

1. With eyes closed and one hand on your heart (spirit) and one hand on your belly (intuition) breathe in your favorite colour, (or any colour of your choice)

2. Feel your body become immersed in this colour, as you hold this breath for a count of four.

3. As you let go of this breath/colour imagine it circling and swirling around your body.

4. Rest for 4, sitting with the colour comfortably around you. Repeat until you feel you are relaxed and calm. When you feel ready, open your eyes and take one more deep cleansing breath.

During this exercise, think about the colour. What does it feel like? Is it warm? Cool? Sensual? Does it have a flavour? A shape? A scent? Is it soft? Bold? Is it Loud? Quiet? What does your heart feel? Can you feel your heartbeat with the colour? How does your heart feel? Do you feel your intuition come alive? What does your intuition tell you?

Now take a sketch book or what ever medium you desire and start creating whatever intuitively comes to you. Do not over think it, just let the creative juices flow. Feel what your body felt about the colour during the exercise. Let the energy from the breathwork direct the art freely. Continue until you feel like you are complete.

You can use this as breathwork/colour/imagery whenever you like for inspiration, motivation and creative genius recall. Try using different colours or images as you desire.

Happy creating Genius!

Evelyn Applin is an intuitive acrylic abstract artist bringing the vibrations, textures and colours of Vancouver Island to her canvases for collectors to experience the awesome powerful essence of West Coast Canada. Being born on the Island she resonates with the rhythms of the Salish Sea and the magnificent surrounding old growth forests that provide her inspirations. She is a strong survivor of domestic violence, the proud mother of 3, and gramma of 7 wonderful souls. Her creativity has always been part of her life and has helped her through many tough times by writing, painting, textile design and theater. She loves animals, especially cats for whom she designed beds and playful toys that supported her family during the tough years. She also now enjoys creating character portraits of cats for loving owners. She is trained in Five Elements Acupressure, Indian Head Massage, Reiki, Life Coaching, Laser Therapy, and Hypnotherapy and is currently studying Artistic Coaching. She welcomes connecting with anyone who is interested in creating life balance, encouraging creative soul expression.

http://instagram.com/rambling_mind_studio

* * *

11

Storyboarding Your Life by Suzanne Jenne

The most powerful creative hack I've ever used is storyboarding. Storyboarding is a technique used for years in film making, advertising, and marketing in order to conceptualize a story and build its progression, while communicating the process to all stakeholders involved and building the project out. But, its application in the personal and creative realm is amazing!

I've used storyboarding to get out of a hole when I am overwhelmed, to design and produce sales training, personal development workshops and art retreats in France. I've used it to write a book, to build a project plan, but perhaps its most powerful use is when I am absolutely, totally stuck and I have no ideas.

You can use it for goal setting, conflict resolution, self-reflecting or you can also use it to solve deep problems or make decisions like:

- Should I move?
- Should I get a Master's degree?

- Should I get a divorce?

To build a storyboard is really simple.

- Start by grabbing some sticky notes (multiple colors if you want!) and some markers.
- Begin by writing out and posting the first idea you have, or the first word that comes to mind if you have no ideas. Pros and cons of a particular path count as ideas.
- Post it on a wall in front of you that is visible to you throughout the day.
- Next, post the second idea or word.
- Continue in this fashion until you have exhausted the words/ideas on the subject; this could take an hour or a week.

The point of the exercise is to get the stuff that is swirling around in your brain, "out there" in some kind of visual representation, where you can more easily organize the information, decide, build your plan and move forward, or not.

Now, go back and start gathering ideas or words into logical groups and look for associations, patterns or themes.

- Is there a process emerging; does something come before other things?
- Is there a hierarchy?
- Is there a logical pathway?
- Does this create other ideas and word associations?

Next, step back and pull it all together. Write statements that summarize the groups and findings. Give this analysis a name, like "Retreat Plan" or

"Decision to Move to California" or whatever it is that this is about. Think about it for a few days.

Last, summarize your "macro" level findings about the storyboard. Summarize in a paragraph, or two, the analysis and the decision, or plan, that has emerged.

Good luck in your storyboarding efforts!

To receive my free ebook, "Get Back in the Studio and Paint," go to suzannejenne.com.

Suzanne Jenne is an award-winning self-taught Artist, Author and Transformational Coach who has over 30 years of corporate experience in organizational change, coaching and sales. Her unique approach to coaching draws from her extensive background in the creative arts, behavioral coaching, change management, and consulting.

With over 25 years of experience as an artist, actor and NPR disc jockey, Suzanne has participated in and produced scores of art shows and creative events. She has facilitated engaging and insightful art workshops and retreats across the USA and Europe since 2000. Suzanne uses innovative, productive approaches to art-making with new materials and creative methods so her clients can get fabulous results!

Suzanne is a certified IIN Health and Wellness Coach, Hypnotic Regressionist, Clear Beliefs Coach and Positive Intelligence Coach. Additionally, she is a skilled facilitator and Master Trainer, providing clients with the knowledge and tools they need to get clear on their life's work.

As a Transformational Coach, Suzanne assists clients in improving their creativity, relationships, health, money, and mindfulness using Clear Beliefs, "Shadow," and Archetype work, Past-life Regression, and art. Her clients have experienced breakthroughs in abundance, success, health and joy through visionary exercises and activities.

If you are seeking greater happiness, fulfillment and results in your life, contact Suzanne to schedule a free Discovery Call at sjenne@suzannejenne.com. Learn more about her unique approach to coaching and how you can have fun while achieving your goals!

http://facebook.com/suzanne.jenne

* * *

12

The Act of Conscious Creativity by Karen French

There are many who don't consider themselves as gifted artistically, so they never let themselves experience the joy of painting. But what if I told you that creativity is so much more? Creativity incorporates the skill of observing, capturing ideas and visualizing, it grants us space and time to do something for ourselves to create something that is uniquely ours.

I'm a flower queen and inspire and empower expatriate women to bloom, to gain a sense of direction, overcome overwhelm and stress. I share techniques and tools to find clarity of purpose by sharing practical achievable steps resulting in fulfillment, so that they too can create their own powerful success stories. I do this through daily inspiration on social media, through online courses and in-person via creative retreats and experiences. Culture shock, lack of work opportunities due to visa restrictions in a host country, loneliness, lack of self confidence, the list of challenges goes on and they are all real to women experiencing life in a new country. The way to combat something negative is to adopt a positive mindset, stop thinking and do something creative. If this is you, then you've come to the right page and today I'm sharing a few things you can do to relieve some of that tension.

As the world's leading wisdom coach Vikas Malkani (my own coach and mentor) says, "Wisdom Is The Stabilizer Of Life." So I ask you to be grateful. Each day before you sleep, recount the day and write down or count in your head 10 things that you are grateful for. They can be as simple as 'Thank You for the comfy bed I have to sleep in' because being grateful for what you have in life is paramount to attracting a life you deserve.

Make a creative date with yourself to do something for you, preferably in nature. Whilst out, take time to observe the small things that you would otherwise be too busy to notice. It may be the pattern on the bark of a tree, a flower, an unusual seed or a shell on the beach. Take simple photos with your phone. When you get home, find some time to observe those photos, write down what you like about them and find one to draw & colour in or paint. Observe how these exercises made you feel.

We're not looking for perfection here, merely the act of conscious creativity. Creativity often sparks new ideas and I love to share ways for you to get inspired, live the life that you want through visualization. Two powerful methods I use are vision boards and mood boards. Let me remind you that we all have great value, we just sometimes need a little help to see it!

Mixed Media Abstract Artist, Silk Painter, professionally trained International Floral Designer, Life Wisdom Coach and Published Author. Having lived as an expatriate child, creative entrepreneur, wife and mother for over 5 decades in 6

countries in the UK, Middle East and South East Asia and faced many challenges over the years as a serial expatriate, I can draw on a wealth of experience to serve expatriate women experiencing Trailing Spouse Syndrome which I prefer to call 'Trailing Talent'. I also serve expatriates who are repatriating and Empty Nesters globally, to bring back their joy of life, to regain their sense of identity and to find a purpose in the next chapter of life through art, nature, creativity and wisdom.

http://www.karen-french.com

* * *

13

Beauty Through Art Journaling by Britt Bjoro West

The number of times I have met people saying "I'm no good at art" or "I'm not very creative" is quite staggering. When I ask why they think so, I can guarantee 9 out of 10 people got their confidence knocked out of them when doing art in school. Many would love to be able to paint, draw or use other creative mediums but don't know quite where to start. And that's where I love to introduce them to art journaling! I believe God created beauty for mankind to enjoy, and there is so much of it in creativity.

Being creative is not complicated or only for a select few. Everyone is invited. It is well known that art brings healing as it allows you to forge a connection between your mind and your body. Unlike exercise, which works your body, or meditation, which clears your mind, art-making accesses both mind and body to promote well-being. Visual art activities have been proven to reduce stress levels and anxiety. There is no doubt: Art is good for us! I was introduced to mixed media and art journaling in my forties and have never looked back.

When my marriage fell apart after 28 years, I was heartbroken and struggled emotionally and mentally for quite a while. During this season I found that art journaling brought me healing and, over time, it helped me to let go, forgive and restore my joy. It also helped me in dealing with the trauma and pain of the rejection that I felt. The use of colours and words, the process of listening to my inner self, to connect with higher powers and to allow myself to be still and just be, brought me peace. I could create without thinking about the outcome; it was more about being in the moment, enjoying playing and what I created was all for me, not to show anyone. It was such a liberating experience. Something magical happens when we put down colour onto paper or a canvas, time and stress seems to disappear as we get to just concentrate on what is in front of us.

For those who don't know, mixed media is a term used to describe artwork composed from a combination of different media or materials; for example, colour pencils, acrylic paints, paper etc. An art journal is the same as a written journal, except that it incorporates colours, images, patterns, and other materials. It is almost like a visual diary where you can creatively express your ideas, thoughts, feelings, memories and emotions through any type of art form you enjoy. One of the great things with mixed media and art journaling is that anyone can do it, no artistic skills or previous experience is needed. I still use art journaling for my well being and as a tool in my creative process. Art journaling often inspires my paintings too. It may be that I get a pattern, an idea or a picture out of the journaling, or sometimes it might bring a release and encourage me to get painting.

My recommendation when you first start art journaling, is to remember that it's not going to be up for display so there is no need to worry about what other people might be thinking of your art. You can experiment, play and do whatever you want. There are no rules in art journaling, just do what feels good for you as this is your space and time. Below is an exercise and a list of supplies to get you started.

The list is just a suggestion so feel free to use whatever art supplies you might have at hand.

- A journal with thick paper (around 230mgs thickness is best to avoid bleeding through the pages, but thinner works as well) or a piece of thick paper/card.
- Pen.
- Acrylic paints.
- White gesso (not essential).
- A butterfly template (free online or cut out from a magazine).
- Glue.
- Paintbrushes.
- Colour pens.
- Scissors.
- Scraps of paper/tissue paper.
- Any crayons, oil pastels, ink or other art materials you might have available.
- Kitchen roll paper and water.

Now, you're ready to begin:

1. First, write down the word "Precious" on the art journal page. Look up the meaning of the word precious, and write these down too.
2. Next cover the page with paint, one or two colours to start with, whilst you think about the meaning of the words. Maybe say them out loud to yourself, and remember that this is what you are: precious.
3. When the page is covered and dry (you can speed this up by using a hair dryer) cut out your template butterfly and stick it on with glue.
4. Colour it in any way you like (paints, pens, pastels, ink etc). If you cover it with gesso first, it gets a different feel. You can stick bits of paper onto the page (tissue, scrap bits, book pages, anything) and paint over them with gesso/paint to add some more texture if you wish.
5. Now make some marks in various colours anywhere on the page. Use the back of the paintbrush to make some dots, paint a couple of little

squares and, whilst the paint is still wet, pull some lines through it with the back of a brush.

6. Circle in the squares with colour pens in a different colour. You can draw flowers, leaves, doodles or any words that might come to mind. Water down some paint or use fluids/ink to drip/splatter onto the page.

7. Press down with the kitchen roll paper to imprint a pattern. Just keep on adding things for as long as you like.

Remember, you have permission to play. You can cover over anything and do layers. Go with the flow. Follow your instinct (trust your instinct; remember we are all creative). That's it! You have now done some art journaling. You can always go back to it and add more at a later date. Hopefully this will inspire you to get more creative.

Finally, my advice to you on how to grow as a creative: Invest in yourself, take courses, join creative communities locally and online. Be aware of your feelings, be kind to yourself and learn to have a positive and abundant mindset. You were made for a purpose, to shine like a star and no one can do it for you. Don't be afraid to be heard and seen and definitely do not compare yourself with anyone else; you are unique and amazing! Koselig!

Link to a free demonstration of the procedure described above is available on my website www.brittbjoroart.com.

Britt Bjoro West is a mixed media artist and tutor from Norway, based in the UK. She teaches visual art in a way that is accessible to everyone, enabling them to use it as a tool for wellness.

Britt Bjoro West is passionate about uplifting and empowering others to be creative. Through art journaling she provides strategies and tools for anyone struggling to be creative and wanting to overcome mindset blocks. Britt strongly believes in the healing power of art and that anyone can embrace it by being shown simple tools and encouragement. She has provided tutorials, workshops and nurtured creative spaces for a wide variety of individuals and groups over the last two decades. Having experienced freedom and healing through art herself after the trauma of a painful divorce, Britt is now on a quest to uncover the fun and beauty in releasing people into their individual creativity. Everything she creates, through her paintings, photographs or tutorials, aims to be uplifting and bring hope. Britt's passion to serve the community through creativity led to the setting up of a woman's art and community group with her business partner Karen, which won an award of £10 000 from the National Community Lottery Fund. Britt has a background as an interpreter and journalist, as well as setting up two businesses. She is now primarily focusing on her art business Britt Bjoro Art, providing online tutorials, memberships and paint parties. Britt has had her art showcased in various local art exhibitions, been featured in the paper Berkshire Live and a guest speaker on BBC Radio Berkshire.

http://www.brittbjoroart.com

* * *

14

Self Expression is Freedom by Candice Jean

The emotional turmoil in our house was real. After 17 years of grooming and conditioning, my now ex-husband was an abusive hurricane of untamed emotions and I took the brunt.

With my emotions silenced, my physical body started to suffer from a debilitating form of anxiety. I had no idea what was happening. I would struggle to talk like I was being choked, I couldn't breathe, I felt nauseous most of the time, constant headaches, I had dizzy spells and I hadn't slept well in years out of fear. I had completely lost sight of who I was and what my purpose was. I had rejected myself and my desires to live someone else's life.

After we separated, I stumbled across human behaviour. This is where I learned how important it was to know your values. Yep, you guessed it... Creativity was my number one!

Art and creating had always come so naturally to me but I hadn't done art in 20 years. So, I picked up a paint brush and just started. I was very rigid at first but the more I leaned into my intuition and let go of the fear to be perfect... it all started flowing.

I feel colour, whether wearing it or painting with it, allows people to express themselves with a deeper conversation.

Every colour I use has been part of my healing journey of learning how to express myself again. I've laughed, cried and even high fived my canvas while painting. It all shows up with no judgment and feels so good to let go. My art has evolved over time, as my self expression has become more authentic and free.

I've realized that within the challenges, our biggest growth awaits. Art has been the missing link for me and it will always be my 'go to' form of therapy.

We were all born to share colour in any form and it has allowed me to connect with my own unique expression. Art is a place of joy that literally calms the mind, body and spirit.

Candice Jean is a colour enthusiast who is excited to share colour that inspires emotional connections & moves energy through the intuitive expression of art. Dabbling in all things creative, including designing homes for over 15 years, Candice has finally found peace on the canvas using her experiences as an unspoken expressive and healing outlet. Being a mum of 2 and rising above a long term abusive relationship, Candice has seen the power of stepping out of

someone else's shadow, being true to self and doing what you love every day.

https://candicejeanart.com/

https://www.bagkandy.com/

* * *

15

Courage to Create—The Way of Peace by Margot Dermody

The courage to create is a transformative experience. It requires embracing vulnerability, finding inspiration and strength in the face of fear, pain, or grief, and being willing to take risks to start new projects. By cultivating courage, anyone can tap into their innate creativity and unleash their full potential. And by tapping into your passions, and what really moves you, you will often find the energy to create.

I love being outdoors, and I enjoy a peaceful hike in the woods. This movement in nature fills me with creative energy. My other passions are the animals that love us unconditionally. Being with them inspires me, fills me with love, and improves my well-being by caring for them. I also like to travel and explore culture, history, and arts in museums and public spaces, which gives me ideas. When you engage in what you love doing, you will discover the motivation to create. It is a satisfying cycle and one of life's great joys.

To build courage, it is important to understand that beginnings can be scary, but they are also full of potential. Whether an artist is starting a new work or embarking on a new creative endeavor, the act of taking that first step can cause anxiety but can be exhilarating too. Taking baby steps and realizing that there is always a new beginning may be helpful. The creative process often begins quickly, gets messy in the middle, and as you finish it slows down. Finding a state of flow through inspiration and activities like meditation and creative exercises can help overcome self-doubt and build confidence.

It is vital to remember that everyone has the potential to be creative, regardless of their background or experience and their choice of artistic practice. Embracing vulnerability and recognizing the power of our own creativity can help us feel alive. However, building the courage to create is a process that requires practice and persistence. Overcoming setbacks and challenges is an inevitable part of the creative journey, but it is through these experiences that we build resilience and the strength to persevere.

There is nothing more satisfying than creating a unique work that is filled with your true feelings and transmits your energy. Finding the courage to create works that represent your authentic self is the way to peace.

Margot Dermody (b. Takoma Park, MD) is an artist based in Pittsburgh, PA. Her current solo exhibition, The Way of Peace, Forward and Back, is in the Pittsburgh Federal Courthouse lobby, Art in the Courthouse, through April 15, 2023. Her work has been shown in numerous exhibitions, Stories to be Told, Art Mum's (2023); Chromatic, PxP Contemporary Gallery, (2022); Stronger Together, Art Mum's

(2022); Alone, Together, the Associated Artists of Pittsburgh (2021); Full Circle, Concept Art Gallery (2021); and the Associated Artists of Pittsburgh 107th Annual Exhibition at the Westmoreland Museum of American Art, (2019-2020). She has also shown in the Pittsburgh Cultural Trust Gallery, William Pitt Union, Gallery One | Collective Works, and the Pittsburgh Center for Arts and Media. Recently, she was awarded Idea Furnace sessions in the Artist Residency Program at the Pittsburgh Glass Center, where she continues to work as a studio artist. Bringing together elements of the natural world with human emotion in painting, sculpture, and photography, her works span a wide range from a neutral monochromatic palette to a more explicitly vivid and affective narrative.

https://www.margotdermody.com

* * *

16

Can Focusing on Others Boost Creativity? by Amber Killinger

C reativity is often seen as an internal process—one that requires time, brainstorming, and perhaps even a little bit of solitude. But what if there was another way to boost your creative juices? What if focusing on others could be the key to unlocking your creative potential? The idea of other-centeredness—focusing on, and caring for, the needs of others—has been gaining traction in recent years. Other-centeredness or being other-oriented is about putting the needs of others first and being willing to go out of your way to help them.

But what does this have to do with creativity? Well, research is suggesting that by focusing on others, we can actually unlock more creative thinking. According to an article published by Washington University, in a set of experiments, people "came up with more creative ideas than peers after they practiced "emotional reappraisal." Reappraisal means reframing an event to reduce the negative emotions you feel. You may not realize how often negative emotions and/or habitual thought patterns can block creativity. It's like you've experienced the same emotions and thoughts so many times, that they have worn a familiar pathway in your brain, much like walking through the same route in a yard wears down the grass and creates a path. Your thoughts get stuck traveling this well-known, comfortable path, making it difficult to veer away and come up with new thoughts and ideas. Our mind gets stuck. When we focus on others, our emotions shift along with our focus. We get out of our own heads, our thoughts change and generally, we feel happier, which allows ideas and creativity to flow. True innovation happens when we're in the flow. Here are a couple of scenarios to help bring this idea to life.

Scenario #1. Wanda decides she would like to redo her front yard. She would like a brand new landscape, and because she is generally a creative person, she was thinking of designing it herself. However, when she goes outside, she stares at her front yard and can't think of any ideas to change it. She has looked at her front yard every day for years and she has emotional associations with her yard, such as hating the weeds, loving a tree, and wishing her flowers would flourish. Wanda is used to seeing her yard as it is, not as what it could be. So Wanda struggles to come up with ideas; her creativity is blocked.

Wanda is sharing her frustration with her friend Suzy, and Suzy says, "I was actually thinking of redoing my front yard too."

Wanda is inspired to help her friend and volunteers to help come up with ideas for Suzy's yard. At Suzy's house, Wanda's mind is flooded with ideas. "We could pull out all of those plants, put a tree here, and here, put a new garden here, and add a walkway between these gardens so people will have an experience as they walk through the gardens and up to the front of your house."

She sees possibilities in her mind and the ideas flow. Why was it so easy for Wanda to come up with solutions for Suzy's yard and not her own? For one, she doesn't have emotional associations or attachments to anything in Suzy's yard, so it's easier for her to think about getting rid of plants or a tree, or adding something new. Secondly, focusing on someone else's problem changes our emotions and thought patterns and allows new ideas to flow in.

Scenario #2. Lisa, a landscape artist, has been experiencing a creative block for several weeks. She hasn't been inspired to pick up her paintbrushes, and she is frustrated that she can't think of anything to paint. While Lisa is out shopping, she bumps into a friend, Brian. While talking, Brian mentions that he's looking for a new piece of art for his living room, and he likes Lisa's style. Lisa starts asking questions, like how large of a painting is he thinking about, what colors are in his living room, and what types of landscapes are his favorites (desert, winter, flowers, etc.). This interaction has changed her emotional state from frustrated and in her own head, to feeling happy about helping Brian and brainstorming to solve a problem. This interaction has gotten Lisa out of her own head, caused a shift in her emotions and thoughts, and allows Lisa's creative juices to flow. Lisa gets a commission for a new painting, her creativity is unblocked, and Brian's dilemma about getting new art for his home is solved.

So you can see how getting out of your own head and focusing on someone else's problem can turn into a win-win for both people. Luckily, this process of focusing on others to help boost creativity can be applied to any job, hobby, or situation, and is available to everyone, no matter your age, gender, or financial situation.

Our focus on others can help us to see the world from a different perspective—one that allows us to come up with more creative solutions. So if you want to be a more creative person, start by focusing on others—and see how your creativity skyrockets in the process!

Amber Killinger is a creative being with a pure soul. Being a neurodivergent person influences her art and her daily life. Her goal is to promote kindness and love through her art, to raise awareness of how many peoples' brains work differently than neurotypicals, and to embrace strengths and gifts that are part of this diversity.

https://amberkillingerart.com/

* * *

17

You Get to Discover You by Sheral Sly

My dream started coming true at 68! I didn't know I had a dream, but my dream came true. What? After the "dust settled"—kids raised, beautiful home, wonderful husband, cute dogs—there was an empty space inside of me, a hole that had yet to be filled. This "hole awareness" started when I turned 65. I kept praying "God I know you have a plan for me."

In all honesty, I thought that I was perhaps being brazen by asking for more, after all, I had been blessed with so much. I would vacillate between being satisfied and grateful for what I had (which I was) and praying I want more. I want that "thing" you planted inside of me, just me, to be realized.

It began with the gift of a bottle of wine. The wine bottle was so pretty, kind of a turquoise color, that I couldn't throw it away. I bought some paint and painted the bottle. At the time I lived at the beach, so I collected some sand, put some in the bottle and then attached a shell. (My mother-in-law gifted me hundreds and hundreds of shells that she collected from her many trips around the world.) I started selling decorated wine bottles and other unique bottles, at the Street Fair in San Clemente. My neighbors were so cute, they would save bottles for me.

One day, I thought about what it would be like to paint on canvas. And that was it, that was the thing, the fireworks and sparkle lit up my soul! I was on a mission! To you the reader, my mission, my joy, my heart, what I want you to hear and believe: Your dream, your longing, your something more is not a thing floating out in space, because you think of it and know it, or you have no idea, it's a part of you and it will bubble up and out will come a great celebration of the discovery of a new part of your life! Just You! The very uniqueness that cannot be duplicated. You've been an amazing daughter, sister, mother, grandma, employee, wife, friend, etc., and NOW YOU get to discover YOU, just you, for You and who knows... the world!

It's like before you have a child, everyone says "oh it's going to be amazing, blah blah blah," for me I couldn't imagine truly what it would be like. I believed it would be awesome, but I just didn't know how AWESOME until my first child was born, and saw him and held him. Then it was real. That's the message I want my art to be.

Encouragement, boldness, seekers, to unleash that feisty, take-no-shit girl you used to be. That girl that with 3 of her buddies on a whim jammed into a VW bug and drove to Ensenada for the weekend, camped on the beach, drank sangria and danced the night away. Actually they only slept on the beach one night, they got a hotel the next night. We were in our early 20's, we were a little crazy, but not that crazy! I remember her so well, that girl was me and is still me.

It's our Time, we are badass and I am grateful to God for his plan. We are going to inspire other badass, searching women to find their dreams come to fruition and the ripple effect will be felt and seen around the world. What joy!

P.S. As of this writing I will be 71 in April 2023. I have so many exciting things that have happened and even more amazing things coming up. This book is just one of them!

Southern California Grandma abstract mixed media painter. A passion for messaging to women; Your dream is real and you are worthy to have it all.

http://www.artbysheral.com

* * *

18

Listen To Your Intuition by Tina Marie Romero

We all came from the same source—the Ultimate Creative who created us all. As offspring of the Creator, we were all born with innate creativity designed for us to tap into to make our unique life into a living masterpiece.

As children, we harness creativity freely. But as we turn into adults, we start to doubt ourselves. Fear and judgment take over our lives and kill our creativity.

The good news is we never lose our innate creativity.

We can always tap into it by Listening To Our Intuition. Our intuition is our Creator's way to bring us back to our inner child unafraid of living and creating the life of our dreams.

Our intuition is our innate creativity's cry for attention, especially when it has not been harnessed in a long time. It is our unapologetic inner child dying to be heard and unleashed.

Listening to our intuition leads us to the life of our dreams. It gives us a roadmap to our life's purpose, a personalized GPS that gives us precise directions.

The problem is 50% of Americans do not know how to listen to their intuition. Just like any skill, it needs to be learned and practiced. Similar to building a muscle, it needs to be exercised often. The more we do it, the better we get at being intuitive.

It took me years to cultivate my intuition and turn it into my superpower. Here are my A.C.T. suggestions to build your intuition muscle:

A—Acknowledge dissatisfaction/restlessness. When something does not feel right, don't brush it off or camouflage it. Treat it as an invitation from the universe that something is wrong and it is an opportunity for you to change something. Keep an open mind and commit to not be afraid of what may come up.

C—Carve time each day to be alone and really listen to what your heart is trying to tell you. The best way is to meditate, pray or take a walk. It can be as little as ten minutes, but it needs to be done consistently every day. You need to mindfully "listen" without distraction and judgment. Be patient. I guarantee you will eventually get a breakthrough and gain an unwavering peace of mind.

T—Take immediate action. When you get clarity on what your heart is telling you, be bold and take the next first step no matter how small it is. The important thing is to do something. Be decisive and do not second guess yourself. Be confident in knowing that the universe always conspires to make your dreams come true if you have the courage to pursue them. Celebrate yourself for taking the first small step.

We only have one shot to live our life. We are commissioned to be the artist of our unique life and given the big opportunity to make it our magnum opus. It is never too late. Start today.

Tina Marie Romero, MBA is an intuitive aging expert passionate about helping others age gracefully, grow bolder and reinvent themselves so they can live their life's purpose.

As CEO of Synergy Homecare of N Central NJ, she helps families by providing compassionate caregivers for anyone so they can stay and die at home with dignity and independence. Her agency grew from zero to seven figures in less than three years and has consistently received Best of HomeCare Provider of Choice and Caring Star Service Excellence Awards.

Uprooting herself from the Philippines in 1995, Tina reinvented herself from a fearful undocumented worker without a voice into a self-made millionaire employing 100+ immigrants, a board member collaborating with business leaders and a lobbyist advocating for seniors and immigration reforms. She was also a cancer survivor whose recovery propelled her to be a triathlete, marathoner, Spartan trifecta finisher, yogi, and dancer.

Tina has been featured on NJ News 12, The Lisa Show, The FilAm, Authority Magazine, Thrive Global, Medium, Life Expressions and various podcasts.

https://synergyhomecare.com/nj-piscataway-08854/

* * *

19

Creativity Can Soothe the Soul by Kitten Looney Bailey

From the moment we are born, we learn ideas that give wings to our interests. The creative industry is an army of strategic thinkers across multiple platforms, it's everything we see, touch, and hear every day. The first step to accessing your creativity, is to evoke emotional intensity to awaken your inner energy that is a mirror of yourself, then reflecting into something creatively. A perfectly executed Rembrandt, Van Gogh, or the grace of a Mona Lisa is not a prerequisite for success. Art is like a cup of tea, but you pour from yourself into what inspires you; let your cup runneth over. Hacking into your creative energy is a powerful tool which opens the channel for energy to flow. When you think of a powerful emotion that deeply impacts you, release that energy into what you choose to create. Combining this action along with prayer or meditation can enable your creativity to reach a higher purpose, especially within the healing arts.

The decades I spent in the advertising industry, began with prayer for each project, putting intention into a design that would achieve the results to give my client the highest return on their investment. As a professional, helping to drive their success was important to me, but adding spirituality to it, manifested greater potential. While I am a spiritual person, I also believe there are many types of spiritually, especially in the creatives and healers you'll find here. They each have the desire to help others and the universe has a divine light within each of us.

Many creatives are blessed with the double-edged sword of perfectionism, the inner conflict that sabotages the very essence of creativity, even Michelangelo would X out his drawings that he considered mediocre. Our creative ancestors blazed a trail for our artistic freedoms that were denied to many, particularly women during the 18th Century, when they began to enter the art scene. Generations of artistic leaders fought to be heard throughout history and the obstacles they overcame still resonate through artists today. Our artistic diversity and unique styles are like a fingerprint, only you can share your soul's imprint. An individual's truth and expression of their emotion can be seen through the vibrancy of a colorful lens and when inspiration meets courage, magic is ignited, and creative energy is given a voice with wings in which to soar without limits.

We were created to share our gifts with the world, and in the words of author Wayne Dyer, "don't die with your music still in you," a profound statement for me, as I've spent the last years battling triple positive breast cancer, none of us know the time we are granted. Inevitably we all have battles in life, health, loss, trauma, divorces, toxicity of people we love, but through it all, we are not just survivors, but warriors as we continue to go forth into the darkness to share the light of ourselves with others. My faith has saved me from the depths of despair, and when tears fell, I turned to my art to help ease the pain, to release the demons that fell upon my shoulders. While not all life's bridges can be resolved, there is a tranquility in creativity that can soothe the soul that aches while also promoting healing.

THE VISION'S PASSAGE

All aboard creatives, a journey's ahead.
Design a vision where dreams are fed.

Jump the train to a far away land.

Let them talk, if they can't understand.

Life is a flame that flickers in the end.

Dance your rhythm, be your own trend.

Fantasy Island's paint is still wet, but use your mind to enter the set.

Believe in the magic of music in the stars, it takes you on paths beyond where you are.

Foolishly follow the Madhatter's lead, going crazy is when an artist believes.

Ride the rocket into the galaxy's ring, feel the rush of sparking your dreams.

Manifest your fortune of gold, let music and painted notes unfold.

Did you create the path you strode?

Did you dance in the moon's lighted globe?

Take the chances, live the vision you see.

Give passage to your authenticity.

Kitten Looney Bailey was born in Brazil to American artist parents, but was considered a native Texan from the age of 4, until her move to Hawaii in 2022 with her daughter Grace and their dogs. Kitten has been an art professional in the creative industry for over 30 years, receiving multiple awards for her work. While creativity is her passion, her personal interests also led her into training in the healing arts of sound energy therapy, Biogenesis healing and aromatherapy, which she integrates into her work whenever she can. Her mission in life is helping others to see their potential and guiding them through lighted energy.

https://www.klbeecreative.com

* * *

20

The Art of Juicing Creativity by Linda Samuels

Picture this: You haven't been in your studio, your art space, your happy place in what seems an eternity. You've found yourself in a creative black hole.

This happens to us all.

Every. Single. One. Of. Us.

Creativity flows in and out as often as a sailor on leave.

Allow me to fill you in on a little secret on how I grab hold of my own creativity. One word. Well, maybe two.

Humor and laughter. For real.

"Laughter IS the open portal to creativity"—said my badass artist unicorn friend.

Allowing yourself to laugh, even when times seem bleak (and believe me,

I've lived a good portion of bleakness in the last few years) creates a natural flow within your body and with that, creative juices start to flow out. It can't be helped!

A sure fire way for me to let loose is to get on the phone with one of my besties. I have a few on speed dial (do people still say that?) and they never fail to get me fired up!

Sometimes, I'm the one knocking them out of the park and other times, I'm crossing my legs trying not to make a mess! By the time that's over, I'm in such a good place that the vibration coming off me starts to rattle my jar of paint brushes.

And herein walks creativity. Being all like... hell yeah... I've been here the entire time. You just needed a kick in the ass. Welcome to your studio.

Humor is mindset at its best.

Linda Samuels is an intuitive mixed media artist who helps people find their inner creativity, by using her own art as inspiration, combined with her quirky sense of humor. Her unconventional method of teaching enables them to step through their fear and tap into their creative flow, so they can become the true artist they know they are.

https://www.ellesseart.com/

* * *

21

The Art of Lunar Living: Using Moon Magic to Unlock Your Creative Potential and Find Inner Peace by Tracy Abbey

Get ready to tap into your creative potential and find inner peace with the art of lunar living! Think of the moon as your personal guide while you embark on a journey of self-discovery and healing. While there are many ways to access this powerful energy, today we will focus on a unique Vision Board process ritual from my "ARTuals with The Moon." I hope that it will bring magic and transformation into your life!

While tapping into the knowledge of the energies of the Moon's cycles and astrological elements and how they affect your daily life, Vision Boards unlock our inner creativity, joy, and playfulness.

By participating in these lunar ARTuals: creating, journaling, practicing artistic expression, and reflecting on our inner selves, not only a fierce act of self-care, but we can harness the Moon's natural healing and balancing energies to bring about positive changes in our life. It's not just about creating art; it's about improving our physical and emotional health and finding a deeper appreciation for the quality of our lives.

Every month we have the opportunity to creatively attune our awareness of our intentions to the rhythm of the lunation cycle. The Moon moves through time and space like a meditative mind in relation to the light of the Sun. When we steadily and willfully accompany this odyssey, we begin to see our potential manifest in a new light. We begin to live in a reality more closely related to the visions being illuminated in our minds as we see them through, every step of the way. So, let's embrace the phases of the moon and ride the waves of this celestial energy. Who knows what magic we can create when we tap into the power of the moon?!

There are eight phases to the moons cycle that it progresses through each month. Each phase has a traditionally commonly accepted energy associated with it. You can use this knowledge to help you get a start to feeling into the specific energies of each phase. Example: new moon for new beginnings and manifesting.

Start With A Moon-Inspired Vision Board!

A vision board is like a visual representation of your dreams and goals. And what better way to tap into the moon's magic than to create a vision board inspired by its energy?

You can make your moon-inspired vision board as simple or as in-depth as you want. Some people even create them electronically using collage-type apps on their phones, laptops, and iPads. The most important thing is to have fun and let the moon's energy guide you as you create this artistic expression of your goals and dreams. Put it up somewhere you can see it and let your visionary board energy infuse into your daily life every time you see it. Take note of anything you put on the board that you wished to manifest, as a goal or future dream, and let's see how quickly those things come into being in your reality.

Making a lunar cycle moon-inspired vision board is a great way to work with the energies of the moon and harness its power to manifest your desires. This activity would best be done when the moon is in the lunar cycle you are wanting to work with so that you can channel that energy into your creative expression masterpiece!

Here are some steps you can follow to create your own lunar vision board:

1. Gather your materials: You will need a large piece of paper or poster board, some magazines or images that resonate with you, glue or tape, scissors, and any other craft supplies you want to use.

2. Set your intention: Before you start, take a moment to set your intention for your lunar vision board. This could be a specific goal you want to achieve or a feeling you want to cultivate.

3. Plan out the lunar cycle: The lunar cycle consists eight total phases but the four main phases: New Moon, Waxing Moon, Full Moon, and Waning Moon are a good place to start. Decide which phase you want to focus on for your vision board, or create a board that encompasses all eight phases.

4. Gather images and words: Look for images and words that align with your intention and the phase of the lunar cycle you are focusing on. For example, if you are focusing on the New Moon phase, look for images that represent new beginnings, fresh starts, and new opportunities.

5. Arrange and glue: Once you have gathered all of your images and words, arrange them on your paper or poster board in a way that feels intuitively pleasing to you. Glue or tape them in place.

6. Add lunar symbols: To enhance the lunar energy of your vision board, you can add symbols such as the moon phases, stars, or constellations. You can draw these yourself or find images to print out and add to your board.

7. Display and use: Once your lunar vision board is complete, display

it somewhere where you will see it often, such as your bedroom or workspace. Use it as a tool to help you stay focused on your intention and work with the energies of the moon to manifest your desires.

Remember that your lunar vision board is a personal and intuitive creation, so trust your instincts and have fun with the process!

So if you want to boost your health and creativity, why not come paint with me and ask me all your woo woo and moon related questions and experience a LIVE ARTual *at Ask Tracy Abbey on Youtube* where I host a weekly painting tutorial, my 11:11 Daily Art on the Witching Hour Segment and other magical activities, sure to delight and spark your creative woo woo side!

In my online creative membership, we do a full moon and dark/new moon ARTual like this each month. So go ahead and let your creativity soar under the enchanting light of the moon!

Blessed Be Tracy ~ The Cats Whiskers Mobile Art Studio ~

Tracy Abbey is a South African-born artist with a natural talent for creating and a passion for expressing herself through art. Specializing in African animals and landscapes, Tracy's formal training began in oil paint and later moved into oil

pastels, acrylics, and mixed media. Her art is not just visually stunning but also promotes healing and inner peace. Tracy offers bespoke commissions, shamanic journey art, and mobile paint party entertainment through her Cats Whiskers Mobile Art Studio and online membership for those seeking to express their spiritual journey through their art. She has received accolades, including a local one-man show and a feature at the Lodi Art Hop in 2022, and is currently working on a book collaboration. Experience Tracy's magical art world for yourself.

http://www.thecatswhiskersartstudio.com

* * *

II

Phase 2: Unlearn & Disrupt

22

Gently Heal What Stands in the Way of Your Greatest Self Expression by Adie McDermott

The most beautiful thing you can be is yourself and yet this is one of the hardest things to achieve. **Let me show you here how you can use the creative process to start to gently become** confident be more of your beautiful self and live a life you love.....

I believe there is beauty in every person, that it is our differences that make us unique and that our darkness (the parts of ourselves we mask and hide) actually make us beautiful **and I see the creative process as a place where we learn to see, accept, trust, love and value the beautiful being that is ourselves.**

How does it work? The creative process itself works as a mirror, therefore, we can use the process to recognize where we are stuck in life, release negative beliefs we have about ourselves and then introduce new positive beliefs based on how we would like to be seen in the world. Used like this it improves our joy in life, our self-esteem, our ability to be successful at what we do and earn more money and….it hugely improves the quality of all our relationships.

The simple act of creating something new (not copying something, or following along step by step), asks us to really listen to and trust ourselves. It takes courage, vulnerability, self-confidence, trust and belief and allowing ourselves to be imperfect. You could say (and I do) it takes radical self-acceptance, a major shift in how we think about and treat ourselves. And… (the best part is) just making a mess on our page and creating for fun, cultivates and nurtures our ability to do ALL these things throughout our whole lives.

Before we begin…

What stops most of us from creating something is 'trying to do the right thing' and our enormous fear of 'doing the wrong thing.' Having to fit in and to know the answers before we begin. Conventional thinking tells us that we need to have highly developed art skills to make any sort of art and practice them for years before we produce anything beautiful. NEWS FLASH! To create something you just need the courage to give up the outcome, give up having to make something magnificent you can hang on your wall and just enjoy the process of creating!

To bring more creativity into your life, and discover what you love, first, before you even put pen to paper WONDER AND WANDER:

1. Be curious: Try new things, question what is true, think of new ways to do and see things, not just what you already do everyday.
2. Pay attention: Creative people observe everything, even and especially the little things. Slow yourself down, so you don't miss the beauty of what's directly in front of you.
3. Be adventurous: Not only take yourself on adventures & try new things, but start to allow yourself to think more expansively.

4. Try new things: Try things that interest you, but also pursue diverse interests. You never know what you may find.

5. Collect information: Read and research ideas, follow other artists. There are thousands on Instagram and You tube. Start with me @artbyadiemcdermott.

6. Go on walks in our beautiful nature or try meditation to develop your abilities to slow down so you can actually hear yourself and your desires, see the beauty that is all around you and develop your creative abilities.

7. Ultimately DISCOVER WHAT MAKES YOU DIFFERENT, what YOU love, as opposed to everyone else, then... bring things you discover into your creations.

Are you ready to try this out?

Create a safe place to start to do this work.

I recommend starting in an art journal that you can close, not a big canvas that anyone can see.

1. Choose 2-3 mediums you like or would like to try. My art journal favorites are watercolor paint, Posca paints pens and coloured tissue paper, but you can use any mediums you have at home... watercolor paints, inks, coloured pencils, paint pens, collage paper, watercolor pencils and acrylics are all great to try. Conventional thinking tells us we need to plan every step of our art so we get it just right. Instead, make an effort to create using your feelings **not your thoughts.**

2. Firstly, and most importantly, give up the outcome. Start instead with a simple scribble, a doodle, making a pattern or repeating a shape, then coloring your whole page in using paint or pencil. You could also start by wetting your page and adding drips or brush loads of watercolor paint onto your page and letting it run to wherever it wants to. These

83

first layers are all about play. Try not to think about or judge what you are doing and instead... Just allow yourself to do the things that come into your head.

3. Build up the artwork in layers of different mediums. Each time you add something new, let it come from you. Be inspired by what's already on your page.

4. Choose a color you like, a pattern you like, an image you like or add something from a time in your life that you loved. Don't overthink or question this... just do it. This part of the process encourages you to listen to yourself, have fun with the process and start to think about what you love, as opposed to anyone else. This is the start of self-expression, making unique authentic creations and bringing your beautiful self to life.

5. Letting your inner child play instead of allowing your mind to analyze and perfect everything creates the most beautiful results. We all have an inner critic or mean girl, hear your inner critic and choose to keep going anyway.

6. Instead of planning everything, this process asks you to tap into your inherent creativity and trust that if you keep going you will eventually create something beautiful on your page. I like to add faces to my artwork and change my creative play, my scribble and expressive mess into big crazy hair or colourful backgrounds; creating weird, wonky women who again share my belief that our differences, our quirkiness and our wonky bits make us beautiful.

Anyone can do this process, ANYONE! But to do it well, requires you to **step way out of your comfort zone.** There is a good chance you will feel uncomfortable being imperfect, letting go of control, really listening to and trusting yourself. GETTING STUCK IS GOOD and in fact, it is where the biggest magic happens. When combined with the holistic healing, belief-clearing and neuroscience techniques I use, it is a process that gently heals what is standing in the way of self-expression: your ability to show up confidently as YOU throughout your whole life.

Adie McDermott is an award winning mixed media artist, transformative art tutor and business coach, and a single mother to an amazingly beautiful neurodivergent, transgender teen. An ex co-dependent (addicted to unhappiness) and a chronic people pleaser Adie understands first-hand the challenges as well as the life benefits, relationship benefits and even the business or career success benefits of learning to be more self-expressive and self-accepting. Combining 20+ years of studying human behaviour, human connection, neuroscience, philosophy with her endless mixed media techniques, she now guides artists of all levels and abilities, to free their creativity, express themselves, love who they are and create a life they love living.

The process here is part of her incredible online creative healing program WHOLE. You can learn more at adiemcdermott.com

* * *

23

Daily Habits Support a Creative Life by Kira McCoy

We are whatever we CHOOSE to be. We create our daily experiences by making those choices. We are becoming more of whatever we have chosen, in every moment. You can be and do anything you desire—all while enjoying the beautiful, powerful, creative, inspiring, freedom-filled, abundant, bountiful, connected and inspired life of your dreams.

You might be encouraged along the way to make bold moves, take big risks, stop "playing small." But I know from the life I've lived that it's those small, daily, almost microscopic thoughts, actions, choices, and movements that actually create change.

Did you know that about 45% of every single thing you do in a day is routine or habit? If you had to think about HOW to put on your shoes or wash your face every time you did it, that would take a lot of mental energy so your brain has adapted to create ritualistic behaviors as a protective measure. This would be great, if you were consciously and carefully choosing which habits and rituals to make for yourself.

Take a good honest look at your life right now and answer these four questions:

1. Did you choose and carefully create your habits?
2. Do your daily rituals support your values?
3. Do you even know what your values are?
4. Can you name your habits, and recognize whether they support your mission in life or not?

If your answer was no, then there may be room for some creative improvements so that you can be empowered to make better choices and stay in your power. Here are some ideas to try incorporating into every day for a few minutes.

Write. With a pen, on paper. Or with a stylus on a tablet. Do not type. Your brain doesn't get the same oomph from typing as it does from good old fashioned handwriting. Don't just document, instead try asking yourself questions. Such as "What is the most impactful thing I could do today?" "What was the most interesting thing that happened to me yesterday?" "What are my three top priorities today?" "What can I say to myself today that would be supportive rather than critical?"

Asking questions to your inner voice will reveal things you might miss if you just write down a diary entry or your shopping list. Don't skip writing. If you can't think of anything to write, just take out a pen and paper and start writing "I don't know what to write but I'm open to ideas and..." over and over until something starts to flow out of you. This is called stream of consciousness writing and you may be surprised what comes out! If you get inspired to take an action, make time to do it the same day.

Make a short, achievable to-do list for the day. If you don't like the task-management sound of that, make a Top Three list—these are the three non-negotiable things you would like to start, finish, accomplish, enjoy, experience, or get done today. Feel the satisfaction of crossing them off the list. We overestimate what we can get done in one day and then we can get self-critical, so take some pressure off by limiting it to three and see how that feels.

Create an Affirmation for the day and say it aloud. This would be an "I AM" statement to support your main goals, priorities, or dream. If "I am" is uncomfortable or sounds too strong or unbelievable, try "I'm working on..." as a way to ease into it. (Example: "I am so creative!" vs. "I'm working on my creativity every day!") Decide when you will say it out loud. You could say it to stop negative self-talk, you could say it to your own face in the mirror when you need a boost, or you could sing it to yourself while driving to work. At some point in the day, say it out loud. Say it with feeling. Absorb it into yourself so you can start believing it.

Move your body. It doesn't matter how. You do not have to get 10,000 steps (in fact research shows 7,000 is enough). You don't have to break a sweat. Movement is life. Movement is nourishing. Find a way to move that makes you fall in love with it. Because like Newton said, a body at rest tends to stay at rest—but a body in motion tends to stay in motion. And ACTION creates momentum to keep taking action.

Take a moment to celebrate yourself. You really are great and you have survived every single thing that has happened to you! Things are OK! You are OK. What are you wonderful at that no one ever tells you? Congratulate yourself for it. Stop waiting for someone else to recognize your greatness, don't give that power away. Celebrate You because you are worth it. Throw yourself a dance party or a private concert in the shower. Celebrate!

Move one thing in your space. Change the energy. Take a look around you in the space you spend most of your time. Is it tired, uninspiring, untidy? Take a moment to make a move. Don't go on a cleaning spree, that's not the point. Move ONE thing and allow the energy to start flowing again. Let that action inspire your next one.

Kira McCoy is an Artist, Author and Coach who uses her passionate curiosity and creative problem-solving skills to create multiple businesses and lead other women to create their own success.

As a former art teacher turned CEO, she has worked on all aspects of business from research and development, to wholesale, manufacturing, printing, online sales, social media management and leading staff. She has survived her share of rainy days, trauma, and childhood wounding, but always chooses to see the silver lining and uses it to shine brightly for herself and others.

Kira is the co-author of a niche best selling book "Polymer Clay Art Jewelry," sharing her unique ideas and knowledge with crafters worldwide. She is also the co-founder of the first podcast dedicated to polymer clay, and has been creating a wildly popular clay-focused YouTube channel since 2007.

https://dailywrituals.com

* * *

Hugo Goes on Holiday! by Katrin Bader

Hush.

Can you hear it? That voice?

Yes, the one that comes from somewhere inside of you, whispering gently what your heart, your soul desires.

Yes?

Yes, but...?

Yes, but there is another voice, a louder voice, right?

It interrupts the other one. It's fiercer, stronger, you've heard it in your own voice, maybe the voice of your mum, your dad, maybe a teacher, a partner, even a friend or society in general? That one tells you not to listen to the other one. That it's just a dream, that it's not possible, that it's wrong, that you are not good enough. It's maybe for others but not for you.

STOP.

That's the voice you have to learn to ignore—even if only temporarily—in order to be free, to be creative, to do brave things, to overcome fear and to be able to turn up the volume of that other voice that speaks from your heart. That gentle voice is your intuition and once you re-learn to trust it, it will be easier to follow your impulses which then create that change that you want in your life.

By definition an impulse is a sudden, strong and unreflective urge or desire to act. However, how often has that other voice called you back in such a moment? Be honest. It's important to know that that loud, strong voice, that keeps you from living your dreams, doesn't mean you any harm. It is your friend. It wants to keep you safe, comfortable, protected, but small. Sadly, this most likely impedes you to grow into your full potential.

So, there are only two options. Learn to ignore it or stay where you are. Which one is it for you? Exactly. And you know what? It is super easy. It's only a matter of practice, as everything in life. I show you how to ignore that voice in order to live fuller, braver and happier. Give that voice a name. Find a ridiculous one, a funny one, if you like, have a laugh at that talker in your head who wants you to stay small. Banter with it. You can joke with him, but make clear that he has no power over you.

Hugo (You go!), to give an example. "Hugo, I am the boss. I say where we are going!" He doesn't like that? Well, send him to the moon to count the stars or to a deserted island to sweep the sand, send him to swipe all the leaves in the jungle or whatever Sisyphean task occurs to you, in order to keep him busy for a while, just long enough so you can do the thing you need to do. I promise it will work. You know why? Because you set the intention. And that is all it takes.

Personally, I admit I haven't heard that voice in a long time, at least while painting. This is proof for me that painting is my purpose in life. Hugo has no power over me when I'm painting. I'm in a state of no-mind. I do what comes through me, there is no voice judging me. It's good the way it is. However, in other situations, this voice keeps showing up. Thanks to this easy hack, however, I have learned to tame that voice. To just ignore it. Simply by sending it away for a while. And trusting whatever comes.

This allows you to follow that gut feeling, to make that bold move in your company, to sling that paint on the blank canvas, to jump into that training, to book that flight, to overcome that fear and talk to that stranger. Try it. Step by step. Impulse by impulse it will make a difference and it will change the way you look at the world and how the world looks at you. Have fun and find your joy!

But what will THEY say?

Just ignore this.

It's typical Hugo talk.

Intuitive abstract artist, certified Conscious Reader, teacher, mother, wish-maker at shooting stars, believer in the good and the potential of everyone, all this and more is Katrin Bader, Austrian based in Spain. She creates bold, bright paintings, guided by her inner voice. Through her playful and vivid art, she shows us that a positive outlook on life is always the better choice. Empowered by having found her purpose with her intuitive art, she inspires and guides others to find lightness

and joy in their lives.

http://www.katrinbaderart.com

* * *

25

Rediscover Lost Identity and Heal With Dance by Jenny C Cohen

To help you heal and live your best life, I want to share a bit about the DISCOVER process: a 10 step framework to recover from adversity by engaging the physical body with the spirit of play, dance and movement.

After my breast cancer treatment, I felt traumatized and completely lost. I found myself unable to find myself in the mirror. I would be at the theater, dressed in full dance costume with all my makeup on, eyelashes and everything, and I couldn't see MYSELF—only the outline of the costume and the outlines of my hair—not my face or my body. My eyes would skirt over my actual reflection and my brain was unable to process it.

I thought I was "being there" for everyone just as I used to. I was actually adrift at sea, completely lost and not even aware of it. I found my way back through and later designed my DISCOVER process to help others do the same.

What makes my company, Dance to Heal Wellness, so different is that we teach and show how to feel safe in our bodies no matter what the day brings.

You can incorporate movement into your daily routine and discover its healing power.

You can uncover buried anger and learn how to eliminate its detrimental effects on your recovery.

We help you find the subconscious processes holding you back, and align your life with your survivor body so that you can love it, scars and all.

Sometimes the life you once knew and loved no longer feels like your own. You have trouble connecting with friends and taking part in any outside activities.

You don't trust this body because it just feels different through trauma, injury, or a medical diagnosis. Few can understand the feelings that keep you from embracing your new body. And so it is possible to feel alone even when you're surrounded by loving family and friends.

We often secretly search for ways to feel "normal" again. You are not alone! I have a process to help people feel more whole after treatment. It is called the DISCOVER process. And while it was created after my journey through cancer, there is a need for this for all of us because the Covid lockdown has been proven to cause trauma on a global level.

I invite you to try the first steps to unlock creativity and healing during your creativity. Acknowledge your perseverance to today. My personal example is "Did I almost die?" and celebrating daily being alive.

1. Tune into your 5 senses one by one to anchor in the present. Smell. Taste. Touch. Hear. See. Start with the most primal and move to the most practical.
2. While maintaining your attunement to all 5 senses, inhale for 4 counts

in your nose slowly and then exhale for 4 counts out your nose or mouth slowly. Focused breath work with tuning into your 5 senses refocuses your nervous system from reactive (flight, flight, freeze, fawn responses) to proactive, from feeling fear to feeling free.

3. Now begin moving. Find a movement you enjoy. I chose dance, but you might choose walking, martial arts, climbing, kayaking, whatever. Just stay in tune and MOVE. The key is to break up the stagnancy and turn it into energy, and when doing that while linked to all 5 of your senses and your breath, you are FEELING that energy while connected to your body. From there explore your creativity!!

I invite you to explore your own unique version of these 3 steps.

For more, get your free copy of my book "Outside In Recovery: Dancing My Way Back to My Self After Breast Cancer" at www.OutsideInRecovery.com

Jenny C Cohen is a bestselling author and creator of a multi-faceted program. After she survived breast cancer, she healed through the very same modalities offered through Dance to Heal Wellness. Jenny is an award winning performance artist, mom who homeschooled her fraternal twins (through IVF) to college, college/elite level sports coach, Occupational Therapist and yoga guide.

http://www.outsideinrecovery.com

* * *

26

A Conversation with Limiting Mindsets by Betsy Sue Stern

A re you stuck? Are doubts and fears keeping you from exercising your creative muscles? Do they hijack your creativity and stifle your process?

Join the club. You are not alone.

So, let's talk and address a few of those fears and limiting mindsets (LM) and then respond with truth. The truth always sets us free, and our goal is to move from a place of fear to freedom. Let's go!

You: I'm just not a creative person

LM: So true! Most of the time you don't even know where to start. Once you do, it just ends up looking like a mess.

Betsy: So, you say you're not creative? You've been creating since you were a child. Think of the silly songs you made up, the snowmen you built, your imaginary friend, dressing up and pretending to be a princess or cowboy. That's all proof you are creative. As an adult, you organize your schedule, cook meals, doodle while on hold and daydream about that getaway vacation. You are creating every day.

You: I have no formal art training

LM: Right? You can't draw a stick figure, never mind paint a still life. Unless you have an art degree you're not a real artist.

Betsy: Well, you're in good company with Henry Rousseau, Vincent van Gogh and Frida Kahlo, just to name a few self-taught artists. A blank canvas has endless possibilities, and you get to decide how to fill it up. Don't worry about trying to create anything realistic or staying in the lines. Finger paint! It's a wonderful carefree way to create without expectations. Close your eyes, dig into the paint and go wild. Abstract, intuitive painting is truly liberating!

You: I don't have the time to create or the money to buy art supplies

LM: That's for sure! There's way more important things to be spending your money on. Besides, you're already exhausted with your schedule.

Betsy: A dollar store box of crayons and coloring book will do. Or pick up a pen or pencil; doodle, scribble, anything. As for time? Put down the phone, turn off the TV and treat yourself to the therapy of creating. You will notice a difference immediately. In the process, you may even find you have more clarity and energy for the rest of your day. What we value, we make time for. Value yourself enough to start creating!

You: I'm too old to start now

LM: I agree! What's the sense of even trying at this point of your life?

Betsy: There's no such thing as too old. Sometimes our last act is our best. Grandma Moses was 78 when she began painting intentionally and her works are sold worldwide and shown in museums. Mary Wesley, an English novelist, published her first book at 70, and subsequently, had 10 bestsellers. The list of late bloomers is endless. I had dreams of being an artist when I was a child; at 60, I am seeing those dreams become a reality.

You: What if nobody likes my art?

LM: Oh, my goodness, 100%. How embarrassing would it be to show your work?

Betsy: You are not creating to make anyone else happy, impress anyone or please anyone. You are creating for you; for the joy it will bring you, for the peace you will find in the process. You are unique and the world will be a better place for what you bring into it.

Will you step up to the challenge?

Betsy Sue is an inspired and compassionate soul with a vision to bring joy and healing to the world. She is a self-taught abstract artist, author and speaker with a heart to bring hope and inspiration to her audience. She has a unique talent

for expressing her vibrant emotions on canvas. Artistic expression contributed powerfully to her restoration and transformation from trauma and abuse. Betsy's authentic vulnerability provides a place of safety where she can serve others out of her love and experience. She has overcome with grace and is an instrument of healing to many. Others describe Betsy as, "radiating light and leading with love." Betsy's mission is to inspire hope through her artwork and stories. Her audience and individual clients rave about the evocative spirit in her work. One of Betsy's creative successes was winning a national contest that earned her family the honor of meeting President Clinton in the Oval Office. She promotes her artwork on Instagram, and she shares her stories on her YouTube channel, "This is My Story."

https://www.instagram.com/_betsysueart

* * *

27

Shifting Out of Overwhelm by Elizabeth Vanderliet

You are the common denominator in every experience of your life. These words have empowered me to learn how to care for myself, and to strive for the best version of me. With consistent action, loving kindness has become the dominant energy of my life. Not in a selfish way, but in an indeed "divine feminine" way, a "Christ presence" way.

What's most important? We need to slow down to speed up! It sounds odd, but it's a simplification of tasks and emotions. Next in line is gratitude. It's the ultimate state of receivership. How does anyone get to gratitude from overwhelm? I believe there is an inner healer in each of us, and we must take accountability in finding our way to that life force energy. I call it going inwards, the healthy kind, not the ruminating kind.

As an athlete and artist, the fastest way I know to get "there" is to get moving or get painting. Changing the brain wave pattern from busy overthinking beta to alpha wave to affect a change in mood or temperament is pertinent. I suggest movement, yoga, walking, cycling, or any exercise that increases oxygen exchange. If that isn't possible, paint, meditate, or work in the garden. The act of creating, in whatever form, shifts our brain wave patterns and can signal a recalibration of our nervous system to calm, the opposite of overwhelm.

When we insist on using the past framework of our history, we conform our future to those same predetermined limits. If we choose those old patterns, we blind ourselves to the limitless possibilities. This is predicated on the idea that what is known is safe, and what is unknown is unsafe. It has been studied and written about for decades.

There is a slight difference now because we are all trying to survive the onslaught of the events of the entire world all the time, every day. To keep up is to go headlong into overwhelm. Slow down to speed up takes precedence in the here and the now! Change what you can and let go of what you have zero control over. Start where you are. You are not behind. Your mental health is paramount for your survival. If you think for one moment that this is selfish, think again.

The journey of learning to love myself has revealed patterns, emotions, and wounds from the past, but they no longer inform my future. I am far more capable of helping others if I am operating from a full cup, creative and inspired. A rising tide lifts all boats. You are reading this book and are already working on change. You are doing better than you think. Slow down, and move through to gratitude. Start where you are. Ask for help. I believe in you!

At four years old, her progress report read, "Beth spends most of her time at the painting easel." Elizabeth has spent a lifetime navigating back to that easel. Elizabeth Vanderliet is a seasoned artist & intuitive. From mountain tops to river beds, the adventure seeker in her loves cultivating energy and bringing it into her studio, whether painting, writing or teaching. Having moved between visual arts and the healing arts over the past 25 years, she has finally landed where she can express herself and serve others best. The thread of healing runs through everything she teaches. Years of working on people physically as a Certified Advanced Rolfer ™, continue to inform her leadership as Quantum Energy Practitioner. Elizabeth loves to work with people in pursuit of self-knowledge, wellness, and, most importantly, awakening the fire within. Your brilliance is beyond doubt and fear; Elizabeth would love to help you on your journey.

https://www.elizabethvanderliet.com/

* * *

28

CHANGE. SEE. BE. The Recipe for Becoming Creative by Jen Taylor

Imagine any three shapes. Place them in a row. Now move them into a column. Now stack them on top of each other. Now balance them up on their sides, all leaning together.

Each time you moved them, you Created. Change IS creation. That is the simple, yet profound truth. When you change something, anything, in any way, you are creating.

So stop with the "I'm not creative" mantra. It doesn't serve you and it's not remotely true.

Can you change something? Anything? Of course you can. And changing something physical is just the beginning.

Imagine those shapes again. Go through the movements again, but this time really SEE them in your mind. Are they more pleasing to you in the row or the column? How does the profile change when you reorder the stack? How do you feel when you finally manage to balance them, each supporting the other?

This is a change in SEEING. The shapes are still the same. The movements didn't differ. So what did? Your focus. The degree to which you noticed the changes you were creating. You create by changing things all the time, but if you don't SEE the change... take it in... accept it unconditionally... you miss the creative spark.

Now take it one step further. This time don't imagine the shapes. BE the shapes.

How can you CHANGE yourself? Shift the pieces of your identity around. Tilt them on edge. Feel that precarious balance of past and future identities.

Now focus in and truly SEE it... Is there a difference in your idea of You as a creator?

Relax, for it is already done.

YOU have changed.

You ARE a Creator.

Jen Taylor is a multi-dimensional artist working at the ever fluid interface of science and spirituality to help visionary artists give form to their feelings. Whether that's by shaping an intricate sculpture with meticulous details and encoded,

intuited messages just for them. Or by creating a custom shaped, multi-layered canvas so they can bring forth a unique artistic vision. Or by showing them the cohesive and clear message they have within the tangle of their Big Beautiful Ideas. Jen can bridge her contrasting talents in a way that will make your dreams tangible. And she cannot wait to see how many lives your inspired creations transform.

https://meticulous-abandon.com/clb

* * *

29

Manifestation Tools to Shift Your Life Today by Anne Almeida

"*Life isn't about waiting for the storm to pass. It's about learning how to dance in the rain.*"—*Vivian Green*

My mom gave me a magnet with this quote after my divorce.

This was at the start of my own self healing journey. And even though it hasn't always been pretty—they say the ickier the shift, the greater the reward, I have learned how to dance in the rain with a big ole smile on my face and that is what I want to share with you. The power is in your mind and in your words. Here's the thing, manifestation is a big buzzword in the wellness space. We are co-creators of our reality and we are manifesting all of the time. And yes, manifestations are absolutely a beautiful thing; counter manifestations are the things that throw you for a loop. When it feels like you're stuck in the muck, when life is not going how you want it to be going, knowing that you're counter manifesting and creating your own reality can feel pretty shitty. I was stuck in this space for a good bit of time. After working with some of the most amazing mentors and powerful manifestors of beautiful realities, I pieced together these three incredibly powerful tools to share with you. Regardless of what you know or feel you don't know, these tools will work for you to shift your life today.

Tool #1: "you are" affirmations. The "I am" affirmations are all over the wellness space. There is a power in repeating mantras. (It's called spelling for a reason.) For better or worse, your subconscious mind is 95% of your brain and holds an even greater power. If you find yourself repeating the I Am affirmations and feel like you're turning blue in the face as it is not shifting how you feel about yourself, your subconscious mind is exhibiting this greater power. Before you get frustrated and dive into a rabbit hole of why am I like this, there is another way—the "you are" affirmations. Look at yourself in the mirror, look into your eyes. And tell yourself, "You are beautiful." Sometimes our subconscious mind needs to hear it from someone else.

Tool #2: "up until now," three magic words. My life used to be the same shit, different day. And at the level of fact, that is exactly what it felt like. Declaring things never work out for me to one of my amazing coaches, Sonia Ovendon, she interjected the phrase "up until now." Ah the beauty of these three magic words. As I declared things never worked out for me, that's exactly what I was declaring to continue happening for me. Remember, there is a power in your words. Declaring "things never work out for me up until now," your mind will start to look for ways for this to be your new truth.

Tool #3: ask the Universe "how will it feel" + gratitude. I used to wake up first thing in the morning searching for monsters. I was so engulfed in trauma and toxic environments, I would wake up wondering what I was going to face that day. My past prepared me well. There were some evil monsters. And then I did the work, I did the healing. I was out of the realm of monsters, but my mind still wanted to keep me safe. Just in case, right? But this just in case was ensuring my days would have these problems. To shift this, I began my mornings asking an open ended question instead. "How will it feel to feel amazing today?" (Insert whatever emotion you choose.) Your mind will look for ways to feel this emotion. Your mind wants to answer the questions you give it.

But we're not quite done yet… the emotion of gratitude is an absolute game changer. I began a ritual of ending my days journaling about the ways my mind answered the question, saying thank you to all the ways I felt amazing in the day.

I am a mom of 5 and a multi passionate creative and healer who helps people see the magic of their too muchness to spark a life filled with love, wonder and childlike joy.

https://www.revolutionarywellness.love/

https://instagram.com/annebishopalmeida

* * *

30

Breakthrough the Inner Creative Gremlins by Perry Janssen

O nce upon a time ago, in a magical place, you were filled with aliveness, light and curiosity. You may remember running into your preschool class with excitement, full of anticipation. The room was filled with colored markers, crayons, stickers, paints, pretend stations, different colors of Play Doh, cool colorful posters everywhere, and tables with the day's crafts. Your mouth salivating with all the options to experiment and freely express yourself.

Then we begin to grow up. The outer critics abound and we swallow their messages and they become our inner voices. Grades get dispersed with the fear of jaws stalking children. Can you hear the "duh duh duh" music bringing the ominous stomach churning as you await to see if you did it wrong? The seeds planted at this time is the start of our inner critic, comparer, and perfectionism choking the life juice out of kids, beginning a new narrative, "I can't—, I'm not good at—."

This is the start of our natural joy, happiness, and uninhibited self being squashed, mutilated, distorted, plucked, pulled and ultimately so deeply repressed that we begin to believe that we are not creative and that only a rare few have talent. The colors in the environment begin to fade as you grow. The energy is being slowly sucked out of kids like a vacuum cleaner hose attached to a body part. Then, one day you are an adult, working in a little gray cubicle with gray walls and gray carpet. Instead of excitement and anticipation for the day, it is replaced with a glass of wine or bingeing TV series at home to take the edges off.

What the H%LL happened? We have taken the color, the juice, the vitality, and experimentation out of life. By the time we become an adult, we have had to repress a certain degree of our curiosity, imagination, creative urges, energy, and ultimately our "Self." Our "Self" and creative freedom has been repressed, stomped on, beaten up, made fun of, shamed, criticized, and wrapped up and tossed in the garbage. Why is this a problem?

This is the magic of life. Colors. Curiosity. Imagination. Uninhibited creativity and freedom. These feed our soul with true nourishment. Depression, stress, and anxiety are at an all time high. Why? People are longing, searching for purpose, and starving for more. The color of life is dimming and there is a trapped wounded creative inside who is forgotten. Full self-actualization and freedom of expression becomes a fear of rejection and not belonging. But the very thing we need to heal, be free, and bring us aliveness is the very thing that is repressed and ruthlessly criticized.

The Creative.

Through Transformational Arts, I have seen people process cancer, depression, intense grief, repressed rage, and self-sabotage. Energy, difficult emotions, and inner confinement can have tremendous breakthroughs moving into joy, laughter, peace, and an excitement for life again. Throughout history, creativity through storytelling, drawings, painting, and music have been a transformative catharsis and a balm to our soul. Creativity changes brain scans, shifts trauma, moves stuck patterns, heals grief, processes challenging times, and ultimately evolves and liberates us. The creative transforms.

Everyone starts off creative. Until we forget. Instead of growing up…we grew away from our "Self" and our beautiful uninhibited imaginative nature. We bought into the outer critics and gremlins and they took residence and became a Greek chorus of directors in your head. This is sabotaging your ability to be you and express your unique self-expression, which is your purpose. This is one BIG reason why we struggle with our emotional well-being. The outer gremlins become inner gremlins and are picking at us everyday. And we believe them.

So how do we deal with these Inner Gremlins and free our life up to create, be our fully actualized "Self" and express who we are?

Here is the first step to freeing yourself up.

The Recognize Exercise

1. Recognize that your inner gremlins were "learned." They are NOT you. We integrate these in our head and let them direct us so we can feel belonging and acceptance.
2. Recognize that these messages and teachings are not the truth. Ask yourself if these are in true alignment with who you really are because they may be hurting you.
3. Recognize that you were creative when you were little and you learned to create the way others wanted you to. But no matter what, KNOW that you are still creating your life right this very minute.
4. Ask yourself, "What do I really want to create?"
5. Recognize that a Greek Chorus of gremlins are potentially sabotaging your life and your unique self-expression.
6. Recognize that your own inner light is trying to get your attention but it may show up as a desire to numb out through screens, alcohol, food,

busy-sickness, or depression and anxiety.

Repressing our unique self-expression is moving from the color of life to a jail of gray. To burst out of that little cubicle jail, we have to Recognize what is keeping us there.

Creativity is one key to being free. One thing I know for sure... the more creatively free someone is the more they are personally free.

Click the link below if you are ready to take the next step to move through the Inner Gremlins. It will get your juices flowing!

Perry Janssen has been a psychotherapist/writer/ artist/ activist for 30 years. She teaches women who are stuck, stifled, or blocked in their scars, old patterns & paralyzing messages heal mind, body, and soul so that they are no longer inhibited by the past and can live a life of confidence, joy, and personal & creative freedom. Learn more about her NeuroCreative Embodiment Method™ to come home to your Self and Unique expression.

http://perryjanssen.com

* * *

31

Money Is Not Evil by Dr. Zerri Gross

M oney is a topic that evokes different emotions and experiences in people. The concept of money was instilled in us at a young age, and we knew even at a young age that having money was important.

Our parents and other family members often have a significant impact on our beliefs about money and our financial habits. The messages we receive from them, such as "money is the root of all evil" or "you have to work hard to make money," can create conflicting beliefs and ideas about money, leading to confusion about how to approach it. Our experiences growing up can also shape our beliefs about money. If our parents struggled financially, we may develop the belief that making money is difficult, and we will always struggle to make ends meet. Conversely, if our parents were financially comfortable, we may believe that making money is easy and that we will always be financially stable.

It's important to recognize that our beliefs about money are not necessarily accurate or helpful. Our financial habits and approach to money are shaped by our past experiences and beliefs, but they do not have to define our future. By examining our beliefs and developing healthier financial habits, we can create a more positive and empowering relationship with money.

Redefining our relationship with money as a tool is a paradigm shift. Money is a tool that can be used for whatever the holder of the money wants. The holder of the tool can have good or evil intentions for what the money will acquire. However, money is neither good nor bad; it just exists to be used as a means of energetic exchange to accommodate means to an end.

Making better choices comes from being laser-focused on our purpose, why it is our purpose, and how to use one of our biggest tools, aside from time, and money, to achieve the life we're looking for. Just because we become super clear and can make better choices because we are focusing on one priority at a time, that does not mean it will be effortless. It's essential to identify our priorities and develop specific goals to achieve them. By examining our bank statements and comparing them to our budget, we can determine what we care about versus what we say we care about.

Ultimately, our relationship with money is an intimate one. As we begin to develop an understanding of how money is a tool, we can then begin to see how intimate of a relationship we can have with money. It's essential to recognize that money is not the root of all evil. The real root of all evil is the intention behind the action. Money can be used for good or bad purposes, depending on the intention behind the action. By developing a positive and empowering relationship with money, we can use it as a tool to achieve our goals and make a positive impact on the world.

Money is a tool. Understanding your process and thoughts about money determines how you can use this tool. Develop a habit to become clear on your current priorities and how your money is impacted by them. Allowing yourself to be vulnerable with your thoughts and processes and allowing others to help literally helps you get to the next level. Clarity on your priorities and goals sets you free from constantly trying to figure it all out.

Fortunately, I offer a Facebook group where I share gems such as this and offer opportunities to grow for professionals that really just want to help people. To join us, click here: https://m.facebook.com/groups/171847108 1635516/?ref=share&mibextid=q5o4bk

Hello, This is Dr. Zerri Gross also known as Dr. Z. I am a Licensed Marriage and Family Therapist, Therapist Whole Life and Time Management Facilitator, Veteran, and Yoga Instructor that has a passion for helping people unlearn their limiting beliefs about money.

I was once like many of you, growing up hearing phrases like "money is the root of all evil" and "money can't buy happiness." It wasn't until I began to challenge these beliefs that I was able to create a healthy and positive relationship with money.

Inspired by my own journey, I wrote the book "Money is Not Evil" to help others overcome their own limiting beliefs and create a positive relationship with money. I understand that it can be challenging to talk about money and that it's often considered taboo, but I believe that money is a tool that can be used to achieve our dreams and help others.

Through my own experiences and extensive education, I have learned how to create a healthy and positive relationship with money, and I am passionate about helping others do the same.

With a background in therapy and a passion for helping people achieve their goals, I am committed to helping my clients overcome their limiting beliefs, develop positive habits, and achieve financial freedom. I understand that money is not the end goal, but rather a tool that can help us create the lives we want to live.

www.GreaterSelf.org/hello

* * *

32

Activating Magic-Passion-Love by Joanne Morton

There are lots of challenges and distractions in our personal and professional lives that can make us forget to relax and appreciate each moment. The truth is that stress will always be a part of life. We may, however, decide how we will respond to it.

My vision is for as many people to FEEL GOOD 24/7.

When you feel good 24/7, you are able to navigate your challenges with ease.

How does one shift their perspective to feel good 24/7? Magic Passion Love will SHIFT YOUR PERCEPTION!

Magic Passion Love is a renewable, sustainable positive energy source found within all of us, when you allow your magic, feel your passion and live your love, life feels good. When shared, wow! The world needs your wow!

Magic is as simple as looking at the mysteries and beauty of life. I feel if one sees the Magic and understands that we are "part" of everything, perhaps we will understand our responsibility to keep the Magic flowing by taking care of our Planet.

Passion is what can drive us to live our heart's desires. Following our Passions and from living one's dreams can inspire others to live their full potential. We are not here for ourselves but for future generations—this should be a priority.

Most important is LOVE. It is important to start loving yourself. For when you love yourself, you are able to love others. We are here to love. Love is the cure for everything including stress!

When your PERCEPTION SHIFTS—this is the opportunity for MAGIC to occur! When your COURAGE SHIFTS—this is how PASSION begins! When your CONSCIOUSNESS SHIFTS—this means more LOVE is flowing into/ through your heart — with more LOVE in your life, you are Happier, Healthier and you FEEL GOOD BEING YOU! WOW! It's that simple. Simple doesn't mean there is no ACTION involved.

Here is my action list to Activate Magic Passion Love!

1. Find appreciation & gratitude in everything
2. Move your body so you can feel your heart beat
3. Be silent to hear the Divine Source
4. Chat with your Angels and Ancestors
5. Forgive myself and others for being human
6. Think & Act positive as much as possible
7. Allow Magic to appear throughout the day
8. Feel Passion in all that you do
9. Live Love proudly
10. Drink a lot of water
11. Relax & Enjoy the present moment

If you need a zip zap of positive energy to tap into your power, say out loud, three times, I allow my magic, I feel my passion, I live my love. You will have the energy to take on whatever challenges that may show up as well as energize the good that is happening too!

Joanne Morton is an artist, speaker, event producer, and community engagement activist. Joanne mixes art, gratitude, laughter, and visualization together to encourage conversation to create action for ourselves, communities and the world.

Joanne's art and experiences help people activate positive energy within themselves so they go from feeling stressed and frustrated to feel relaxed and motivated. She is currently working on building the "World's Largest Hanging Mobile with her immersive community art experience, "Manifesting Mobile." Since 2010, Joanne has traveled to 17 states to exhibit the large scale hanging mobile. She invites communities and organizations to add visionary art circles to the hanging mobile that reflects their positive visions for the Planet, People, Prosperity and Peace.

Joanne has been producing events and creating art since the 1990s. She has produced monthly art fairs, variety shows and coordinated events for several nonprofit media art organization, including the Savannah Earth Day Festival. She combines her artistic inspirations and work experience to create events that respects, empowers and celebrates everyone.

www.joannemorton.com/freegift

* * *

33

Open-ended Art Play by Sheryl Siddiqui

My name is Sheryl Elizabeth Siddiqui. I am a mixed-media artist. I have a colorful, modern take on flowers and nature-inspired art. Art has had a special place in my life since I was a small child. I had a natural ability to create things with my hands. Art was a form of expression I could rely on when I had many emotions and did not know how to process them. It was a secret world that was all mine.

Creating art would become a vital part of my healing and a tool for calming my mind when I could not handle intense emotions. It was like a form of meditation before I even knew what meditation was.

As an adult, I meditate for at least forty minutes daily.

When I was learning to paint with watercolor as a teenager, putting the brush on the paper was my meditation. It carried my mind away from the thoughts of the day. I would be very focused on the lines of the drawing to create a flower, then the tiny strokes with the brush to create the petals. This focus would be very calming for me.

One of the best kept secrets about art is that it can be so simple, yet we often overcomplicate it. I did not know in my twenties that art would become something that would be there for me at every part of my life journey. Mixing colors would always soothe me, and applying paint to the canvas or paper would always feel so good. Creating colorful paintings uplifted my mood.

The premise of open-ended art is a simple concept that I have incorporated into my everyday life. I have only positive things to say about this fun art practice and I am excited to share it with you.

You will need some inexpensive sketchbooks that stand up to acrylic paint and mixed media. Heavy weight acrylic paper pads, crayons, markers, or pencil crayons to have short free play sessions.

There is no actual finishing goal and no pressure to have a final product. Working on multiple pieces of paper, or recycled paper bags, which are handy for short periods, is ideal. Ten minutes or even faster is fine.

It's time to stop if you start to fuss, overwork, or overthink the art. Here are good rules to follow. No expectations, no self-judgment, and it doesn't matter if you finish anything or ever show anyone the art.

I scratch into the paint with popsicle sticks, write words, use plastic forks, and scribble with paint brushes. I thin out paint and dribble it from plastic containers. I also bought inexpensive student-quality paint that I could liberally apply on the paper care freely.

As this fun little project has continued, I have expanded the supplies to include glitter, modeling paste, markers, gold paint, gold Leaf, alcohol inks, paint pens, and oil sticks. Use a paint roller or try a silicone kitchen tool you picked up from the dollar store.

You can even paint with your non-dominant hand. I often stand up and get far away from the canvas with a long paintbrush, so the brushstrokes are less predictable. Squirt heaps of paint out on your canvas even though you have no idea how things will turn out. True joy and excitement are right within the random marks and imperfections.

If you are going to try this out for yourself, your biggest challenge is going to be to leave your self-judgment at the door. It makes no difference if you are a seasoned artist or a beginner; the important thing here is how the art process makes you feel. That might be a massive switch for you, and if so, that's good. You are tapping into something new.

Open-ended art play is a fantastic way to dissolve any limiting beliefs you may have as an artist. This method will break down any limitations in your art practice. It supplies never ending ways for you to approach your art. Playing with art supplies like you are a kid is the perfect way to deconstruct or unlearn rigid art beliefs. I have acquired many skills over twenty years as an artist. Playing freely with some inexpensive materials started to break down my mental confinements and limitations that I had placed on myself. Stepping outside of the box is exciting and liberating. The art that flows onto my sketchbooks is unfiltered, imperfect, colorful, and beautiful. Sometimes it isn't lovely, and I don't care because that's how I figure out what I love and don't.

This open-ended art process I have described works best when you choose inexpensive art supplies. You can do this type of art anywhere. You can even put the art supplies in a Ziplock bag and throw them in your suitcase when you travel. The last time I went on a cruise with my family, I brought my little bag of art supplies and a sketchbook, and it was so much fun. It also helped me to feel less disconnected from my art process when I returned home. I was even creating art at the airport. You do not need anything fancy. The more basic the art supplies, the better.

Remove any programming, critiquing, or evaluating as you are creating. Let go of the idea of being good art or bad art. You are just freely creating and expanding your ability to play.

125

The real gold in this process is finding what brings you joy in your art and helps you feel calm. You can look over the pages of your random drawings, sketchbooks, and scrap papers and determine what you love the most. Please consider incorporating more art play into your life. Having a constant companion in art has changed my life in beautiful ways. I jumped at the chance to collaborate and be a part of this book to share my experience with others. Art can be a process of continual discovery and exploration. It has been with me throughout the ups and downs of my life as a continual and constant partner.

Open-ended art is just for the pure joy of creation and exploration.

Sheryl Siddiqui is a mixed-media artist who creates captivating wild gardens, flowers, and nature-inspired art. Her focus is to share her love for large-scale art on canvas and the energy of color with as many people as she can.

As the sole owner of Sheryl Siddiqui Art, Sheryl has expanded her business to include digital art illustration. She is an international award-winning artist and has been featured on CBC Radio Morning. Sheryl has a Bachelor of Arts, in Political Science, from Carleton University. Sheryl is dedicated to guided meditation and is a certified Usui Reiki master.

https://sherylsiddiqui.com/

OPEN-ENDED ART PLAY BY SHERYL SIDDIQUI

* * *

34

Enjoy the Space In Between by Shannon Heap

I've only ever known chaos. The trauma and shame that generational alcoholism, domestic abuse and violence creates is insidious—if left unchecked, it will seep into everything you do and become everything you are, but you have a choice, you always have a choice. You can let your tragedies define and control you or you can learn and grow from them, and that will catapult you out of the darkness and into the light.

I am an artist. I AM AN ARTIST.

It took me a long time to introduce myself like that.

I felt because I am completely self-taught, have no degrees after my name or any formal training that how dare I have the audacity to call myself an artist…but I am. I've always known it. Ever since I can remember having independent thought, I knew I had a different way of viewing the world and I tried to express myself in as many ways as I could. I'm a bit of a rebel and don't heed what others tell me. I never believed in limiting myself. Creativity is infinite, why would I handcuff myself to only one skill or concept? Perhaps it stems back to the need to keep busy and find something to delve into to take my mind off the horrendous stuff. I could drift into a world of my own and close out the chaos swirling about me.

Fast forward to today and I am painter, a mixed media artist, photographer, metal/silversmith and jewelry designer, a fabric and textile artist, I make soaps, salves and healing oils and tinctures and I am a reclaimer of old furniture and found objects, just to name a few.

It may seem fractured and complicated to outsiders, but it works for me. It seems every year I think I've figured out what I love to do the most, but then I find something new about a process or stumble across a happy accident and it sends me off onto another journey.

How can we overcome trauma triggers and stress?

How, in this time do I find inspiration, a way to tune in, connect to creativity?

How do I find that magical feeling that sends electricity shooting through me and makes my synapses explode with fireworks?

Well, I actually slow myself and my life right down.

When we move through life too quickly we diminish those glorious moments where we're not trying to achieve anything. Enjoy the space in between… think of even the simplest thing as breathing… that pause between inhaling and exhaling. There is infinite possibility and beauty in that quiet, stillness.

I believe strongly in slow living, slow fashion… slow art. Recover, reclaim, re-use, re-imagine.

I am a forager and gatherer and take as many trips into the woods as I want, and absolutely when it's needed. I did not realize that moving back to the area I grew up in, would make me see how fast my life was going by and I was simply just existing and not enjoying it. Small town living is in itself slower living, however one does not have to live in a small town to experience it.

Make a conscious effort to unravel the minutia you catch yourself up in.

1. Become un-busy.
2. Spend time in nature, by water or sit amongst the trees. In fact, rest against a tree, lean back, and close your eyes and listen to all the sounds around you.
3. Observe nature. Watch the birds, or bees flitting from one flower to the next and when was the last time you took your shoes off and walked through the grass barefoot or sat on the ground? Do it, you'll be better for it. And while down there, stare at the ground and observe all those little creatures moving around that you had long forgotten inhabited this earth along with you.
4. Dig your hands in the dirt and smell its intoxicating aroma. It is easy to appreciate the little things in life when you actually stop to pay attention to them.
5. Notice your breathing and heart rate slowing down, your mind clears and becomes an expansive place, receptive to so many ideas.
6. Don't wish away your past or fear your future. Take all your energy and put it into something meaningful to you.

Creativity is endless and the pleasure of sweet, simple moments can weave joy and happiness into the darkness—we just need to refocus—be mindful, and shift to gratitude and delight.

Hope really is everywhere if you just look for it.

Make what you love not what you think will sell or be popular. Make it with one media, or many. Hell, make it in as many different ways as you are drawn to do! When you're inspired by something, your creativity will flow magically. Trust me.

I do things my own way. I take the long scenic route. I take the time to smell those flowers or make that pie from scratch, or watch that leaf gently drift down to the ground… and I feel the rain. I believe in making mistakes and not beating myself up about it. I own up to them and move on, and I also believe in forgiving myself. When you're uncertain, and doubt your world around you, the clarity you are waiting for is in the actions you're not taking. So take that damn action! Just one step. And then take another… and then another. It may be scary as hell but that means you're doing something that matters.

And above all, share love and kindness. Spread it far and wide and with wild abandon. Be courageous and have the audacity to believe no matter the darkness around you…light can still run wild in your soul!

Shannon Heap is an artist residing in British Columbia, Canada. She is a multi-faceted creator who is always searching and finding wonder and beauty in what would seem to be 'ordinary' things. She is inspired by nature, her environment, and art making experiences where all the senses are used. She shares joy through her work and helps people fill their homes with beautiful creations.

https://instagram.com/urbanheap

* * *

III

Phase 3: Clear & Release

35

The Magic of a Letting Go Box by Amy Lynn Johnson

My all-time favorite Life Hack for Creativity has to be my "Letting Go Box."

In my experience, it works wonders for just about everything—including that pesky inner critic that keeps so many people away from doing creative things they love to do.

Let me explain.

We all have times when we are filled with doubts about our creative abilities. We also have worries and concerns that can take all our attention even if there's nothing we can do about them. I used to spend lots of precious energy worrying about so many things over which I have no control—other people's problems, situations or circumstances that were out of my reach. My "inner critic" would even shame me for trying to paint or create when difficulties were afoot—even when there was nothing I could do about them! I developed a terrible habit of negative self-talk that kept me from allowing myself to draw, doodle, paint or even explore.

Eventually, I stopped being able to create anything at all. I wanted to feel better. I was tired of being "stuck" and unhappy, tired of not being able to draw or paint anything. I began paying attention to my inner thoughts and realized how negative they were. I noticed how often this worrisome and critical inner talk ran through my mind on auto-pilot, repeating the same old phrases over and over.

I started to question these negative thoughts. Were they really true? Did I really think that? I discovered that I did NOT agree with those thoughts anymore—and most were certainly NOT true. I decided I could and I would learn to "change my mind." I found that just by writing the words and phrases down on little slips of paper, they lost some of their grip on me. I could see them more clearly and I didn't believe them anymore.

Then I got a little box, like an old jewelry box, and I started putting the thoughts I wrote down into the box. I declared to myself a New Intention: these negative thoughts no longer served me! I placed all my worries and problems into the box, signaling my decision to LET THESE THINGS GO! I wrote down the same problems as many times as I needed to, and put them in the box as many times as I needed to. 10 times a day? Yep. 30 times a day? Yes! I was determined to set them aside.

Whenever I get something troublesome on my mind, I jot it down on a piece of paper and put it into the box. When it comes back to my mind throughout the day, I remind myself that I've done all I can do—I've placed it in the Let Go box, and I have decided to turn my attention to something more positive. I can focus on something more productive, more creative for right now. I can let myself feel positive in the present moment.

I discovered I can Let Go of worry and negative, critical thoughts—I can put them all in the box, where they can stay—and I can be free to show up more fully for the life that's right in front of me.

Learning to Let Go isn't easy, but it's the most rewarding technique I use for getting my creative life back.

Amy Lynn Johnson is a mixed media artist who teaches "The Art of Letting Go."As creator of The Artist's Oracle System, her work helps others feel guided in exploring their own creativity and intuition. Amy's program has been used in recovery settings to help women discover healing in artistic expression aided by recovery principles for personal growth.

https://www.facebook.com/amy.johnson2022/

* * *

36

4-7-8 Breathing Technique For Creativity by Rachel Bush

L et's turn on your parasympathetic nervous system and help you to feel less stressed or anxious. By using this technique, we will regulate the stress hormone Cortisol in your body, which controls your fight or flight response.

Pranayama is an ancient yoga practice of strengthening the connection between mind and body. Dr. Andrew Weill, who is an internationally renowned physician, refers to this technique as a "natural tranquilizer for the nervous system." Practice four breath cycles twice a day to improve heart and lung functioning, lower heart rate, lower blood pressure, improve immune functioning, decrease pain, and improve concentration.

1. I invite you to find a comfortable seat. If you are comfortable I invite you to close your eyes.
2. I invite you to put your tongue behind your front teeth and relax your jaw.
3. I invite you to breathe in through your nose to the count of four.
4. I invite you to hold the breath to the count of seven.

5. I invite you to exhale through your mouth making a whoosh sound. This technique is particularly relaxing as it exaggerates the exhale portion of the breath.

You have the power to feel a sense of control by simply counting your way through these five steps. This easy technique will bring you into the precious present and force the mind to stop wandering or racing.

My name is Dr. Rachel Bush. I am a survivor, Clinical Psychologist, trauma informed 500 hour yoga instructor, nature photographer and intuitive multi-media artist. I help everyone who is brave enough to ask me for my help on their mental health and wellness journey. I help people of all ages heal, grow and trust their choices in order to live with vitality, creativity, gratitude, beauty, laughter and health in order to make the world a better place.

http://jacobshollowstudio.com

* * *

37

Using Creativity as a Tool for Self-Love & Inner Healing by Rebecca Rosas

Creativity can be an amazing tool used to process and release emotions that come up from challenging situations, triggers, heartbreak, grief, and more. When you find yourself in a situation where lots of emotions come up, take a break. Grab your art journal and supplies,* and try the process below. It will nourish your emotional well-being and it's a great addition to include in your self-love practice. Learning to do your inner work helps you take responsibility to manage your own emotions. You then become empowered and develop a deeper self-love that helps you handle any challenge that comes up in life because you have a way to process and release all that doesn't serve you. When you take care of your emotional health you live life with more peace, ease, and love.

Let's get started.

Step 1— Recognize Your Feelings:

Start with a mixed media art journal and some acrylic paint. This will work with any art medium you prefer. Be sure to set aside some uninterrupted time for yourself. Open up your journal so that the two pages are side by side. Ask yourself, what emotions are you feeling? Write down those emotions on the left page of your journal. Are you mad, hurt, angry, sad, super emotional, feeling sensitive, confused, alone, rejected, mistreated, ignored, embarrassed, betrayed, or humiliated?

Connect to your body and describe what emotions are coming up for you. When you are done writing them down, grab a few colors of paint and place a few dabs on your palette. Choose colors that connect to how you feel. If you feel sad, try using blue. If the emotions feel heavy, you can use dark colors. Take a brush and start moving paint on top of your words. You can add a second color and use your paintbrush to start making marks on top of, around, or mix in with the first color. You can then move on to any additional colors that you would like to add.

While you are moving your brush across your paper, imagine the energy of those emotions moving down your arm, into your brush, and onto your paper. Be intentional with your brush marks. Try expressing yourself with short marks, long marks, zig-zag marks, dots, dashed lines, thick lines, thin lines, boxes, swirls, or circles. Whatever resonates with how you are feeling. The goal here is to bring awareness to what you're feeling and be intentional about releasing those emotions. Let the paint dry and move on to the next step below.

Step 2 — Journal & Connect to Your Inner Child:

On the right page of your journal, turn on some instrumental music and start writing your thoughts on paper. Describe what happened or what caused you to be upset. Ask yourself, "Why do I feel the way I do?" See if you can pinpoint where your feelings are coming from. Ask yourself, Was there another time that I felt this way in the past? Is this a trigger or a pattern showing up in my life? Or is this a unique situation?

Ask your inner child (visualize the smaller younger version of you, age seven or younger) what does she need right now? If she needs love, visualize hugging your younger self. Visualize loving energy wrapping around her like a blanket and filling up her heart. Next, write a love letter to your inner child. Tell her you "see" her. Validate her feelings so she feels seen and heard. Tell her you are there for her. Tell her how much you love her. Comfort her, nourish her, and do your best to give her what she needs. If any tears come up during this process, know that it's ok. Let them flow. You are loved and safe.

Step 3 — Shift Your Mindset & Affirm Who You Truly Are:

When you are done with the letter, add some affirmations about yourself on the same page or the next page. The purpose is to validate yourself in the present moment.

I am loved. I love and accept myself. I am beautiful. I am worthy. I love my big heart. I am kind to myself. I forgive myself and learn from my mistakes. I allow myself to feel deeply and appreciate all parts of myself. I am grateful for myself and all that I have. I believe in myself. I choose me. I love the person I am now and who I am becoming. I radiate love.

Write down any affirmations that resonate with you. When that feels complete, paint the energy of the positive feelings from your I am statements. Choose any colors that make you feel good. Bright and happy colors reflect positive emotions. Paint them over your letter or onto the next page. Connect to those emotions and feel those affirmations to be true. Once done, you are complete.

Notice how you feel. Did you have any realizations or aha moments? If needed, continue to journal your feelings or situation. Notice if there was a shift between when you started and when you finished painting your positive emotions. This process helps you release and process those triggered or heavy emotions. Shift your energy and mindset to more positive, feel-good feelings and give yourself the love you desire. Happy Painting!

Supplies — mixed media art journal, marker, pen or pencil for journaling, acrylic paint or other medium (white and black plus a few darker and lighter colors are recommended, whatever fits your budget), cup of water to rinse brushes when you change colors, paint palette (or palette paper or a paper plate), paper towels to wipe off excess water or paint from brushes, a few different sized paint brushes (bristle or brushes for acrylic are fine, inexpensive brushes work great for this project).

Rebecca Rosas is a Divine Feminine Empowerment & Creativity Coach, Abstract Artist, Creative Entrepreneur and Energy Healer that inspires and uplifts others to do the inner healing work to shine their light. She empowers women to use the healing power of creativity to express their emotions, heal their heart, connect to their feminine energy, deepen their self love and raise their vibration. Her approach helps women see their unlimited potential, align to their true soul essence and illuminate their soul. She is certified as an Usui/Holy Fire® World Peace Karuna Reiki® Master & Creatively Fit™ Art Coach and trained as a Soul Coach. As a creative entrepreneur she has a background in marketing & advertising.

https://www.instagram.com/illuminatewithbecky/

* * *

38

Love Your Fear by Rodine Isfeld

When was the last time that you gave your fear a great big hug?

Most of the time, fear is an uninvited guest who we try to ignore and shove out the door, or stuff in a backpack and hide it at the back of the closet. Let's face it, we are busy. We are strong and we don't have time to let fear get in our way. We have things to do. That was me. A tough as nails survivor who had been slamming the closet door in Fear's face... for years! Heck, when it mysteriously showed up, I'd tell it I saw it and walk through it like it didn't exist. I learned the hard way that, when it has been silenced for long enough, it gets loud enough so that it can't be ignored anymore.

It might be as simple as feeling tired, like you need a mental break and some distraction. Maybe it's a little procrastination or avoidance. Perhaps moments of dread, nervousness, restless energy or a racing heart. I was such a master of 'pushing through the fear', I pushed myself right into debilitating anxiety attacks and a leave of absence. As I was trying to clean up the fear-laden disaster that had become my life, an amazing woman gave me a piece of advice that saved me and changed my relationship with fear forever.

Initially, I thought it was odd and, honestly, a little scary, but it turned out to be so powerful, I want to share it with you. "Love Your fear." You may be asking how on Earth do you do that? Here is a guided visualization you can try.

Find a quiet place, get comfy, relax by taking in a few deep breaths and close your eyes. Invite fear to come and join you. Just let it show up the way it needs to (it's different for everyone). Notice the size, colour and movements. It may appear like an animal or have human characteristics... or it may be none of those. It might feel hostile, but it may surprise you that it is docile or fearful. Remember, no matter what feelings might be coming up for you, you are safe.

Talk to your Fear. Start by telling it how much you love it. Let it know that you see it and that you know it is here to keep you safe and you know that it has been protecting you because it loves you so much. Don't censor what you say... let it all flow and talk from your heart.

Observe: Is it communicating with you? Does it change in any way? If it was large and dark, is it becoming smaller and lighter? If it was threatening, is it softening and relaxing? When I have guided others through this, they often told me that it started out huge, but as they spoke to it, it did shrink.

Keep sharing whatever pops into your mind and when you feel comfortable, invite it to come to you for a hug. It might need some convincing, but don't stop. As soon as it is in your arms, really embrace it. Hold it close, comfort it, tell Fear how much you care about it and how important it is to you. Feel your love pouring into Fear and surrounding both of you.

Let your hearts connect. This can be incredibly powerful and emotional, and you may feel a release of emotions along with tears, (I cried like a baby), and that's OK! In fact, it's beautiful! When you feel ready, let your Fear know that YOU are going to take care of both of you now. You appreciate everything that it has done to keep you safe, but you are strong enough to take over. Your Fear may need some convincing but know that you ARE ready to be in charge again.

Gently release your Fear, let it know it is always welcome to be with you and you are always there to give it a hug… whenever it needs one. How do you feel? After the first time I did this, I felt such massive relief. I had the first stirrings of peace, hope and the belief that I could take care of myself. That I could heal. Fear still ran around like a small child frantically trying to avoid any disasters, but over time, and with many, many more conversations and hugs, I stopped feeling like I had to chase after it. Many of us believe Fear should be avoided or shunned because it is unworthy or, even worse, unlovable.

In my experience, Fear loves us so much that it does everything it can to make sure we are safe, especially when we feel overwhelmed and not in control. By learning how to love my Fear, I was learning how to love myself… ugly bits included. Now, I still have days or moments when my little Fear tries to run wild, but they are becoming less frequent. In fact, Fear has changed, matured, softened, and is now (most days) one of my biggest cheerleaders.

And to think that it all started with a hug.

Rodine Isfeld is a teacher and Internationally published intuitive artist who uses her intuition to capture the majesty and mystery of the Northern Lights. Rodine

is a co-author of an International Best Seller, "Women Standing Strong Together Vol. 2" where she chronicled her journey with depression and severe anxiety and her re-discovery of joy through art. She believes that, by learning to love the parts of ourselves that we think are 'unlovable' we create a gorgeous space for Divine creativity.

When she is not creating magic and messes in her studio, you will find her avoiding housework by puttering with biz work or enjoying time with her grandsons. She is also a lover of bonfires, plaid shirts and coffee!

http://www.rodineisfeld.com

* * *

39

Art: A Pathway Through Grief by Dawn Bova

I rekindled my love of artmaking after experiencing excruciating pain. Grief is a subject you may not feel comfortable talking about. I find this is especially true when the loss involves a child.

When a child passes on before parents, it's unnatural. It defies the natural order of life, and just thinking about it sends shivers down your spine. You may hear, "I'm so sorry, I don't know what to say." And as the grief-stricken mother, I often didn't know how to respond. Bradley was such an inquisitive little guy, always pushing boundaries, taking dares, and making people laugh. His witty personality sucked you right in. He was a charmer with a deep, bellowing laugh and beautiful blue eyes. The void I experienced after losing him to an accidental overdose is indescribable.

Then I met Brian, his sponsor. Intelligent, resourceful, and kind. He walked me through the darkness with his unwavering faith and compassion. He became another member of our family, another son. Two years later, he also succumbed to the insidious disease of addiction. I was lost. How could this happen... again? Shortly after losing Brian, I sat at the kitchen table and painted my heart out. It wasn't a masterpiece, but it was full of love and while painting I felt serenity and peace I hadn't felt in a long time. The painting captures the essence of a beautiful life once on earth, now everywhere. That painting holds such a profound meaning and energy, I will not part with it.

Faith is such an important aspect of life. Learning to trust God, the Universe, Energy, and yourself can be a difficult task when life's circumstances roar like thunder. The act of making art creates a conduit to stillness and serenity. It's in the quiet moments we receive the positive energy abundantly available. In the recovery community, connection to a higher power is a key component to sustained recovery.

Art is a powerful tool that can help you sort emotions and provide quiet moments to connect with your higher power. I believe art is underutilized in all aspects of education. Especially if you are seeking a better way of living. One technique I find extremely healing is infusing a "secret message" into art. There are several ways you can include your own secret massage. Write a note to the universe on a canvas and paint over it. You can write a love letter to yourself on collage paper and incorporate it into the art. I often tear my collage so some words are visible, but the message remains my secret. Scribbling your message illegibly as a design element is another way to create a secret message.

When vocalizing the story or description of your artwork, give hints about your secret message and people will connect with your art. But more importantly, you will connect with your art and permit self healing when words are often inadequate.

When you put YOU into the art, the art radiates an irresistible energy and people are drawn to it (even if you feel the art isn't your best)! I've experienced some of the darkest places. I miss my boys, but use art as a pathway through grief. Learning from the darkness has taught me there is light on the other side.

Practice art, write your secret messages, and have faith you will emerge as a beautiful bright light.

Creating an emotional experience with art is my superpower and I believe you can do it too!

Dawn Bova is an internationally published artist, teacher, and soulful light illuminating her innermost emotions with intuitive painting. Her art has been featured in MADS Art Gallery, Subkit, and she is a co-host of the Art Infused Life Podcast. Her passion is helping those who seek recovery from substance use and grief with the power of art.

http://dawnbovaprints.com

* * *

40

The Art of Healing: Threading Color and Words by Connie Doe

The gift of paints, pencils, and paper offers a simple yet releasing experience for women in trauma.

Words overlaid with paint opens space for women impacted by trauma to restore a sense of self and empowerment. Words meshed in painting allows what needs to be healed to surface in layers and in its own safe and wise time.

Connie created a word/art process that has become a part of her healing programs. She found that along with regulating the nervous system, one of the foundational pieces of healing is to understand and release old beliefs that want to run the show.

Step 1: Offering women poster paints, watercolors, sketch books, pencils, and brushes. The process begins with a list of limiting beliefs where clients take ownership of what beliefs are holding them back. Setting the intention of letting go, they write those limiting beliefs on sketch paper, sitting with emotions that come up in the process. They then take poster paint and cover all those old beliefs which are now hidden under their "art work."

Step 2: After completing several sessions around old stories and beliefs, Connie offers a second word and art project to help clients begin to resonate with the power of letting go and creating a life of all things possible. Beginning with watercolors, sketch paper and pencil, the women are invited to sit quietly and begin to imagine their life a year out. They write on the sketch paper as if they are living in that space right now. Words flow, hope arises, joy comes forward, and trauma begins to release. The women then take watercolors and paint over the words, creating art.

The beauty of this is that the words shine through powerfully, offering clarity and hope.

The Art of Becoming
www.conniedoe.com

Connie is a believer. A believer in life, self love and in all things possible. A survivor of domestic abuse and years of trauma that follow, Connie chose to believe there was a way out.
She believed in stepping into the unknown world of healing and guiding other women to heal was her passion and purpose in life.
Through many years of studies, training, licenses and certifications all in the quest of healing, Connie created THE ART OF BECOMING, a unique healing program that offers programs and community to women impacted by domestic abuse and trauma.

As women step into the healing work that THE ART OF BECOMING offers, they go from living in complex shame to a life of self awareness and self love. It offers a place of safety to be in community, a safe space of vulnerability, courage, honesty, non judgment, healing and hope.

She sees the courage and power in women that have moved from victim, to survivor, to thriver.

As we all walk together to heal, we begin to heal the world.

Through her deep purpose and passion, Connie has founded GIVE TO HEAL.

A non profit for women and by women.

Offering holistic healing service to these women impacted by trauma.

The beauty of GIVE TO HEAL is they offer these healing services at no cost to the women who so deeply need them.

Please visit GIVE TO HEAL at http://www.givetoheal.love

Coming up in 2024: Connect and Become Group Programs and Your Journey Home, an online self paced program.

http://www.conniedoe.com

* * *

41

Focused Breathing Technique to Calm Anxiety in 5 Steps by Catherine Catterson

C ountless people suffer from anxiety. That anxiety not only hinders creativity, but holds them back from achieving their true potential.

Focused breathing is an effective way to stop anxiety in its tracks and give you back control. The beauty of this technique is that it can be done anywhere, and anytime you need it. By adding a second to each breath, hold, and release, you're allowing your body to gather up a bit more of your anxiety and let it go. By the fifth breath, your body and mind have regained their control.

1. Close your eyes and for one second, breathe in as fast and deeply as you can. Hold this breath for one second and release the air in your lungs as fast as you can in one second.
2. Count to three.
3. For two seconds, breathe in as deeply as you can and hold for two seconds. Release all the air in your lungs in two seconds.
4. Count to three.
5. For three seconds, breathe in as deeply as you can and hold for three

seconds. Release all the air in your lungs in three seconds.

6. Count to three.
7. For four seconds, breathe in as deeply as you can and hold for four seconds. Release all the air in your lungs in four seconds.
8. Count to three.
9. In five seconds, breathe in as deeply as you can and hold for five seconds. Release all the air in your in five seconds.
10. Count to three.
11. Relax.

Catherine Catterson is a multi-faceted intuitive composer, musician, and photographer, who helps people take control of their anxiety, fear, and stress through meditative music, visual art, and focused breathing, so they can live their best lives. Catherine has suffered from anxiety, social anxiety, and depression from an early age. As a self-taught musician of multiple instruments, she found her voice through playing music. She started composing her own music as a teenager as a way to calm her anxiety and depression and regain control of her life. Her journey as a photographer began after inheriting her father's camera. She loves landscape photography, as it brings her joy as she captures the serenity and peacefulness of nature. Catherine has released several singles including "Falling Snow," and "Do I Ever Cross Your Mind" on her website and social media platforms, and had her first photography show in the first quarter of 2023. Catherine looks forward to publishing her first children's book in 2023.

http://www.catherinecatterson.com

* * *

IV

Phase 4: Take Risks & Ignite Creativity

42

How to Stick To Your Creative Practice
by Kathryn Snell-Ryan

I'm not quite sure about *your* dreamy visions, but most of mine include some version of the *maker* part of me. It's here that I notice small and strange beauties, where I really see. I'm wearing messy studio clothes, mind wandering, sketches laid out like roadmaps, marks clear and confident. **I am lost in the very best way.**

This dreamy version of me *does* exist, but for way longer than I'd care to admit—hardly ever. Despite falling in love with making in my teens, obtaining an undergrad degree in sculptural Fine Arts, and graduating with a Master's in Art Therapy from one of the most prestigious art schools in the nation—adulting went on to squeeze the creative life blood out of me.

I yearned to make, could smell the clay, kept my sketchbook barely semi-active, had brief bouts of art production that didn't last, dreamed of 1,000 versions of a perfect little studio. **And yet my daily bandwidth just couldn't stretch far enough. I am only one person, my child's only mother, responsible for half my family's income.... You know the drill—21st century living leaving the well of creativity bone-dry.**

I've had a couple *dark nights of the soul* grieving what felt like the loss of an artful, unscripted life. **I grieved a wandering mind, the space to dream, having a vision in mind and artfully seeing it through to the end. I grieved simply noticing, feeling in awe, the sweet ache of recognizing something beautiful.**

The thing is, as a Creative there is literally nothing else that can fill the place that art-making satisfies in us. Nothing. We can either leave that part of us gnawing and empty or we can *make* so that we feel like a whole person.

A few years ago, after reaching creative rock-bottom, I finally figured out how to stick with my creative practice at this stage in adulthood. And it didn't involve a beautiful light-filled studio all mine, or hours of unrushed time, or even feeling inspired. **The secret ingredient turned out to be... TIME and making art with others at a scheduled time each week. That's it.**

So alas, once the power of making with others sank into my weekly cadence, holy smokes the relief was SO REAL; I was *finally* making room in my life for creativity, and it wasn't a fleeting passion project abandoned a few weeks in. **Drawings were getting started and finished, scarves were getting made and gifted. And the weight of that aching disconnection from my creativity vanished.** Not only was I feeling more plugged in to artful living, but my energy on the whole was freed up as I was *finally* tending to an important part of my identity—my maker self.

So if I impart one hack or tip here to get you started on the road to infusing your life with much-needed creativity, let it be this—make with others regularly, schedule that time in and protect it, and show up EVEN WHEN you're grumpy, tired, or uninspired. Our creativity is available to us even when we're not in the mood, even when we're tired or overwhelmed.

Whether you're making with a few neighbors, gathering with old or new friends on Zoom, or joining me online in MAKE—**let the connection and presence of others help hold you accountable to your creativity.**

Your life will undoubtedly be all the richer for it.

Kathryn Snell-Ryan, ATR, LPC is a Maker and Art Therapist fiercely committed to getting Creatives back to the art of making. As the Founder of MAKE, an online Art & Crafting Collective, and a veteran Creative Psychotherapist, Kathryn is deeply versed in the art of helping disconnected, ridiculously busy, or aimless Creatives get back to their craft. Kathryn, a long-time Maker herself and a Graduate from one of the nation's most prestigious art schools, eventually found herself creatively empty as she navigated the endless complexities of adulthood and parenting. Thankfully, the gnawing discontent she felt in the absence of her art-making led her on a path of dogged research and a "create-what-you-need" trailblazing mentality. MAKE, the online Art & Crafting Collective Kathryn founded, has helped hundreds of Creatives who have drifted from their practice get back to their love of making. At the heart of MAKE is a creative community, playful curiosity, and a commitment to the endless beauty found in artful practice.

https://www.mapinsideout.com/make

* * *

43

Future Gratitude to Elevate and Manifest
by Lisa Winston

I f you've been trying to manifest for what seems like forever and have given up, I've got something of a miracle for you. And trust me, I'm one of those people who feel like they were born on the negative side of the bed, so when I tell you this is where the magic happens, please believe me.

Over the past 15 years I've tried many processes, and then, about 5 years ago, I found one that knocked my socks off. I honestly consider it to be supernatural. It's called Future Gratitude and lots of people are doing it. It's more powerful than meditation, visualization, and for me, even better than journaling!

If you want to elevate your energy, create good vibes, and rev up your co-creation machine, spend a few minutes daily playing with future gratitude and watch what happens. Not only will your mood improve, but you'll begin to feel more alive. You'll feel the power of possibility. And the more you do it, the faster you'll see results!

Future gratitude is a little like time travel. You jump ahead to the future, imagining you've already received what you've been wanting and then, PLAY in the deliciousness, in every joyous emotion that comes from BEING IN that story. Future gratitude lights up your cells. It strengthens your immune system, makes you feel happier, and more connected to life. It's a great tool to use when you're feeling stressed, depressed, or powerless.

When you practice Future Gratitude, it becomes fun and easy once you get the hang of it.

1. First, think about what you'd like to create. It could be anything from better health to receiving more money.
2. Next, think about how your life will FEEL once that creation has happened.
3. Finally, write, record yourself, or speak about the entire scenario out loud, like you're experiencing it, savoring it, and absolutely overwhelmed with joy and gratitude for it!

Personally, speaking it out loud seems to ground it in the body faster and gives it more power. For example, one of my dreams is to own a huge art studio, flooded with light from floor to ceiling windows and a breathtaking view of the ocean. To practice future gratitude, I would start by saying "Oh my God, I'm so happy and grateful my dream has come true! I feel the sun on my face as I paint, and I'm completely at peace watching the sun glisten on the water!" And on and on, in as much detail as possible. You want to feel goosebumps as you say it!

Again, you don't want to think the future scene or describe it; you want to pretend you're talking to your best friend about the intense feelings of gratitude for your dream coming true!

BE THERE! Be excited! Be detailed! Generate feelings of massive gratitude until you're practically crying with joy! Allow yourself to be completely immersed in this playground.

Commit to doing future gratitude often and watch your life and body change. You'll also be amazed at the synchronicities that show up to take you to your next steps along the path of creating what you want. Co-creation at its best!

This process works and is what led me to write my own #1 international bestseller, find my soulmate, attract a sporty BMW, and create my art business.

If I can do it, so can you. All it takes is knowing what you want to attract, using your imagination to tell a future gratitude story SO REAL, so exciting, it must show up!

Remember, you have superpowers, so just let go and have fun!

Lisa Winston has been a watercolor artist most of her life. She is a professional vocalist of 40+ years, TV show host, inspirational speaker, author, and mom. After collapsing with neuro-Lyme disease in 2019, Lisa decided it was time to stop "working" and instead, devote her life to creating soul-inspired, high energy, intentional abstracts that fill people's sacred spaces with gorgeous color, good vibes, and JOY. Lisa now primarily creates acrylic fluid art and mixed media abstracts that are infused with high frequencies and messages. She is receiving rave reviews from her collectors, who are experiencing emotional healing and forgiveness, spiritual guidance, and even prosperity after receiving their art pieces.

Lisa lives outside of Austin with her soulmate and life partner, Dr. Joe Vitale, and their puppy, Cabi.

https://art.lisaawinston.com

* * *

44

Be B.R.A.V.E.—A Daily Practice to Jumpstart Your Creative Process by Linda Balliro

"*Sometimes you have to play a long time to be able to play like yourself.*" This classic Miles Davis quote holds a tremendous lesson about creativity whether you're a musician, painter, writer or anyone following a passion to create. But, what does it mean "to be able to play like yourself?"

Playing, or painting or writing like yourself sounds simple, but anyone who has faced a blank screen or a blank canvas has found out that it's more complicated than you would think! We sit down, driven to create some beautiful, or powerful or expressive of something that can't be named, but suddenly the path becomes overgrown with thickets of fear, doubt, confusion or even dread. Everything may seem impossible. You may not be able to find a way to begin, or you get stuck in the middle surrounded by a dense fog. You may create some beautiful notes, or thrilling colors but you can't find your way forward.

When this happens to you, it's usually because you haven't found the way to "play like yourself." This is the most difficult part of the creative process! And yet, your authenticity, your courage to show yourself in your music, art, or writing, is the "secret ingredient" that makes your creative work powerful for you and the world!. Without enough of "you" in those notes, or words or colors, you'll always feel like something is missing.

But just like an archeological search for the perfect diamond, you're going to have to dig a little to find "you," investing time, energy, persistence and practice until that authentic expressive quality that is your unique diamond shines through your work.

Just remember that finding your diamond can be fun! Learning to "play like yourself" doesn't have to be a struggle. In fact, when you have tools and strategies, dusting of the dirt and crafting your art is one of life's greatest pleasures. That's why I created the the BE B.R.A.V.E framework. To give you a tool you can use everyday to guide you through the path to learning to play like yourself.

Be B.R.A.V.E.

Use this Daily Practice to jumpstart your creative process:

1. BELIEVE.
   Everyone has heard the voices in their head saying "what if" or "maybe I'm not good enough." But those voices aren't reality, they're just a collection of neurons firing off together because of past experiences. This is your "mindset" – a collection of neurons that got wired together because they fired off together so often! Fortunately, you aren't stuck with them because your mind can be molded and shaped throughout your entire lifetime. Believing in yourself and your process is actually the natural way your brain works! Your neurons will be quite content to change the way they fire, thanks to dopamine. Dopamine is one of the most important neurotransmitters in

our brain, and believing in yourself, your vision and your creative process, encourages the dopamine systems to function well. Negative thoughts are the unnatural ways that your brain learned through the outside world.

2. RELAX.

Our world is full of pressures and responsibilities. Self-care has become something we have to schedule on our calendars. But, practicing relaxation is vital to building the energy and focus you need to be creative. Build your relaxation practice intentionally. Without it, you can play wildly, but you'll struggle to play like yourself!

3. AWARENESS.

You know the saying "you don't know what you don't know?" This is especially true about ourselves. You can't be aware of every process happening in your mind because there are too many, but you can develop your awareness of your emotional triggers, your physical sensations and your mental blocks. Your sense of your own thoughts, behaviors and actions will fuel your creativity. Taking time every day to build your awareness will give you the clarity to fill the blank pages.

4. VISUALIZE.

Human creativity is boundless because we have the capability to see in our minds eye (even blind people can do this). The human need for shelter evolved into stone castles, lovely homes or high rises because someone could see it in their mind's eye. The knowledge and skills came second. Practice "seeing" what you want in your mind's eye!

5. ENJOY.

If you love what you do, you should be enjoying it, right? But when you're struggling, holding onto the weight of the world or analyzing every step you take, you've forgotten that the creative world should be fun! Remember to enjoy your journey, so even the stumbles along the path will not keep you from your joy!

Linda Balliro, BM in Voice, New England Conservatory, and MSC in Applied Neuroscience, 2023, author of "Being A Singer: The Art, Craft and Science," has been training singers and voice teachers all over the world for 25 years. Associate Professor of Voice at Berklee College of Music, course creator for teachers, singers and creatives, including "Master Your Mind: using Neuroscience to master your mental health and creativity" and "Transform Your Stress: eliminate overwhelm and learn to embrace a new stress-mindset." Ms. Balliro has lived in Europe and the US, performed as a classical soprano, trained students, young performers and nationally touring artists. Along the way, she's learned a few keys to unlocking stress-free creativity.

http://www.lindaballiro.com

* * *

45

Widen Your Community to Increase Your Creativity by Joanne Enders

C reativity is a valuable trait in today's world. Helping individuals solve problems, generate new ideas, and produce unique and innovative solutions. Creativity can't be developed in isolation. Instead, creativity thrives in a community that is diverse and open to new ideas. Widening your community can have a profound impact on your creativity. When you interact with people from different backgrounds, cultures, and experiences, you'll expose yourself to new perspectives and ideas. This exposure can spark your creativity by expanding your thinking and providing you with new ways of looking at the world.

Ideas to widen your community to increase your creativity:

Exposure—One of the most significant benefits of widening your community is exposure to new ideas. When you interact with people who think differently from you, you gain access to a wealth of knowledge and experience. This exposure can inspire new ideas and push you to think outside the box.

Collaboration is a powerful tool for creativity. Working with people who

170

have different skills and expertise, you can combine your strengths to create something unique and innovative. Collaborating is a great tool to bounce ideas off others and see their reactions, to help you refine your ideas.

Inspiration—Widening your community can also provide you with inspiration. When you see what others are doing and achieving, you can feel motivated to push yourself and strive for more. Inspiration can come from anywhere, and being open to new experiences and perspectives can help you find your muse.

Diversity is an essential aspect of creativity. When you interact with people from different backgrounds and cultures, you gain a greater understanding of the world and its complexities. This understanding can help you create work that resonates with a wider audience, is more impactful, and is heartfelt.

Challenge assumptions—When you widen your community, you expose yourself to different ways of thinking. This exposure can challenge your assumptions and beliefs, forcing you to re-examine your perspective. This re-examination can lead to new insights that can push you to explore new creative avenues.

At the end of the day, widening your community can have a life-changing impact on your creativity. Exposing yourself to new perspectives, collaborating with others, finding inspiration, embracing diversity, and challenging your assumptions and view of the world, can help you become more creative and innovative. So, step into this huge world, meet new people, and just see how your creativity can flourish.

Joanne Enders is an internationally sold abstract and digital artist. A published artist, teacher, and community builder, she works worldwide with artists of all genres. Joanne is the host of a weekly space for artists to connect, share ideas, learn about different cultures, and build their communities.

http://www.itsltlthings.com

* * *

46

Practice Intentional Joy by Shari Alyse

I spent the first half of my life running.

If you would've asked me then, I would've told you that I wasn't running from anything but rather I was running to everything. And it was a half truth. You see, the things we repeatedly tell ourselves become the stories and beliefs we adopt until those beliefs no longer serve us or imprison us. I was a chaser of my dreams. I wanted to see the world, experience new people and have lots of adventures. I wanted to start over in new cities when old ones became too dull and I wanted to be in relationships with people that challenged and excited me.

What all of that translated to was a restlessness within and an unconscious desire for chaos because it was what I knew. I had become accustomed to it. At the same time, my soul yearned for expansion and joy and knew deeply that there was another life, a different experience that was possible for me and I wanted it more than anything! I was just unsure how to bring these parts of me together to dance in harmony. How could I have an exciting life but a healthy one? How could I be in a relationship with people who inspired my mind but took care of my heart? How could I find contentment and adventure while staying still?

I relocated to multiple cities, started multiple careers, began and ended multiple relationships and took off halfway across the world for an entire summer to find the one thing that I had always been looking for—me. During those three months of solitude (I didn't know anyone or speak the language), I no longer had distractions or anything to busy me. I had hundreds of thousands of moments to be with me.

And the truth was, it was so hard! And, it was beautiful and life-changing. During that summer, I discovered myself and I discovered my joy! And it had nothing to do with anything or anyone but ME. The greatest thing I've ever done is make the decision to take the journey within. That trip within is your direct route to joy.

People spend lifetimes trying to find joy. They run aimlessly trying to accomplish, achieve and attain things that will bring forth this feeling but there is no-thing that will do it. Except the connection with yourself. Joy is found in connection with yourself. It's ignited when you're fully expressed! It makes its appearance when you're living in alignment with your truth. It floats in when you gift yourself with your full presence in this moment. It shows up in your gentleness with yourself, in kindness to your body, on a walk in nature and your gratitude as you draw breath. Joy envelops you when you allow yourself to fully engage in what you love. It holds you as you listen to the stirrings of your soul and it shoots you out of a rocket when you say YES to the things that peak your curiosity.

The thing about joy is that you don't need to pursue it, you just have to allow it. And I know that it can seem scary to begin that journey within, as we all have things that we might not be ready to face. But just like those monsters we used to be afraid of in our rooms as kids that disappeared when the lights came on, the same happens when we stop running from ourselves and our own light. I no longer need to tell the story that I was running towards everything because as soon as I stopped running, I realized that everything that I was ever looking for was already right here with me. The journey back to myself is where I found joy and your joy is waiting there for you, too.

Here are some fun ways to practice more intentional joy!

1. Say YES to the whispers
2. Connect with nature daily
3. Dance more
4. Blow bubbles
5. Decorate your spaces with bright colors
6. Spin in circles like a kid
7. Spend time with people that live intentionally
8. Be more curious
9. Be more creative
10. Find meaning and purpose in your work
11. Smile more
12. Be gentle with yourself
13. Lighten up

And don't forget, you don't need to change who you are, achieve anything or have anything in order to live your most creative, connected, and joy-filled life!

Also known as America's Joy Magnet, Shari Alyse is a 2x TEDx speaker, bestselling

author, TV host and media personality who is on a mission to reconnect people back to their joy. Shari is regularly featured as a guest expert on ABC, CBS, FOX and NBC and is the host and producer of the TV show, The Joy Spot which features high profile, spiritually connected thought leaders.

http://www.sharialyse.com

* * *

47

Create Consistently to Birth Something in Your Life by Elizabeth King

We are all trying to "birth" or "create" something in our lives. For some it is a business, for others it may be a relationship or a family. People ask me how I was able to conceive 3 children naturally over 41. A significant part of that was because I believed in the ability of my body to create.

You will want to think of pregnancy as creation, creation of a human life. My mantra was "I can create, I am able to create." I did this for even 2 years before I had met my husband and knew I would eventually be having children. Having faith in the knowing is a large part in anything we are setting out to birth or create in our lives.

I then went on to recognize that most people are wanting to create something in their lives whether it is a business, a relationship, a book, or a family. They are wanting to express and to experience their creativity. They're wanting to experience their dynamic connection with the essence of the divine, in whatever way you define that for yourself. The greatest way people may know how to do that is through conception and giving birth to a child. But there are tools that will help you get to that conception and birth that I will share with you. These tools can be used in the same way for anything you are looking to bring into the world, not just a child.

Someone who is truly wanting to be a parent is actually wanting to create. To feel the flow of God, Divine or Universe in creation through them.

Begin to engage in any form of creativity as consistently as you can. It would be even better, even more effective if you're doing this in different ways.

For example, you wake up in the morning and you put on a song that you like from your favorite playlist. You dance around, you move and groove for one song. You're expressing your creativity with movement. If you play a musical instrument, you can spend time doing that. Feel into what your intuition is guiding you to do in the moment.

Then, once or twice a week, you might spend some time doing automatic writing. This is simple, you put your pen to paper and ask a question of the universal oneness and let it be written through you. Pay very close attention to what comes up for you in your automatic writings. Are there any signs or answers that you were looking for that you didn't know you already had within you? Or an awareness that has come up for you to pay attention to?

Sculpt a piece of clay or Play-Doh. Take a piece of clay or Play-Doh and put it somewhere where you might have your morning coffee or tea. In the morning, take this little Play-Doh or this little piece of clay out and sculpt something. Anything. Take two or three minutes. You may make a little snowman. Then you put that snowman on the table or your desk and it's with you for the day. Then in the morning, you will crumple it up while you're having your cup of coffee and you'll sculpt something else. Maybe you'll make a heart or a rainbow. Make it fun. Make it easy. That creation gets to stay with you then you crumble it up the next morning, and you start again. There is no pressure here.

Choose something that is interesting to you. Something that you can be consistent with. If you don't want to paint, then I don't want you to learn how to paint, but if it interests you, fantastic! Creating in some way each day is a beautiful way to show up in the world and demonstrate that you can birth something in any form. What I would like for you to do is to choose at least one creative outlet that you could do every single day, even for 60 seconds or two minutes, like dancing to a song, coloring in a coloring book, making a recipe or sculpting with Play-Doh.

What this will do is very simple—the dance, coloring, sculpting, etc. each will take you less than about three minutes usually, unless you get really into it. It's something simple that you can put into your daily routine. It will begin to let the creativity flow that must move through you. It is also an activity in which you're not attached to the outcome to be amazing because you don't expect yourself to be Michelangelo or the next finalist on the latest TV dance competition show. You can just dance and let yourself move. You can just sculpt something here, and know that it is temporary because you're going to sculpt something else tomorrow, so it just is allowing, it's literally channeling the creative flow through you with the intention that you are able to create in any way.

Many of the individuals who come to me, who are wanting to get pregnant, who have not yet, have stopped playing in their lives. In one form or another, they have become very serious, intense, focused, cerebral, and they've stopped having any sort of playful nature in their life. Consciously and subconsciously you will want to connect back to the play. If you begin to play first, then the souls and spirit babies are excited. Those spirit babies are eager to come to parents who are wanting to play, but these days, very few souls are wanting to come to teach their parents or the world how to play. So get out and play your little heart out!

Visualize the future:
This is so powerful when you are looking to create a human life, create

your family or business.. If you are looking to create a family, everyone has their own vision for what they would like their family to be like, live like and love like, etc. The more you can get specific about where your future baby will be sleeping, eating, playing and visualize your car with a baby car seat in the back with your baby strapped in. Take that visualization further by writing it down and reading it every day and set an alarm on your phone if that is helpful. Create a vision board to lock in that vision for your future so you can go back to something tangible. If it a business you are looking to create you would be specific and very detailed for that industry and who you are looking to serve and support in the world

Tap into your feminine energy:

Most women now are living quite masculine lives without really even noticing how or when they started living so far away from the feminine energy within them. We all need masculine and feminine energy both within us but when you are creating a life you want to focus on the beautiful feminine essence within you. This may look different for everyone but you can try out some of these options and see what makes you begin to lean into the feminine energy more. Put on a dress or a skirt, add some make up each day and some earrings, and get into a practice of receiving. Allow people to do things for you no matter how small and know that you are in your feminine energy when you are receiving. Step outside during a full moon and let the light wash over you knowing that the moon energy is feminine energy. There are a lot of ways to tap more into the feminine, have fun with it and you can even add it to your playlist.

Connect with mother nature:

Experience the beauty that is around you as you simply walk out your front door. Walk barefoot on the earth. Notice the beauty in a flower or tree that is in nature. When we focus on beauty it's very rare that you notice a beautiful flower and think "I wish it was a different color;" you stay with that beauty and staying in that focus is a magical place to be in. Take notice of the natural creativity in nature and how effortless it is. The acorn seed creates an oak tree and is part of effortless nature. You also are able to create in many ways and setting that intention to create a pregnancy or a family is possible.

If you are looking to get pregnant or build your family I teach the four foundational aspects. There are four foundations in my **Creation Continuum**™ to help families create life. All four have a part in the path to creating the family whether you are planning to conceive naturally or with Artificial Reproductive Technologies.

The four foundations are:

1. Medical
2. Mindset
3. Wellness
4. Feminine

Medical in the sense you want to make sure you are in good health and everything in your reproductive system is working as it should.

Mindset is keeping yourself in a healthy state of mind throughout your process of conceiving.

Feminine as we spoke about above and keeping the feminine energy as the primary energy of your divine essence.

Wellness, keeping mind, body and soul in a place of self preservation during this sacred time and doing all the things that can create the wellness within like the consistent creating each day, womb massage, acupuncture, etc., and having support on your journey from family, a coach, etc. so you know you are supported and not alone.

Elizabeth King is an International Certified Fertility Health Coach, Master Certified ICF Life Coach, Birth & Bereavement Doula and New Parent Educator. Her mission is to help people of all backgrounds conceive a healthy baby and carry to term. She had her 3 children over 40 and supports clients through natural fertility, infertility, IVF, miscarriage loss, early pregnancy PTSD, and new parent support. Her practice is based in Irvine, CA but serves clients worldwide remotely.

http://www.elizabethking.com

* * *

48

Dance Party by Jessica Lane

Movement changes our body's chemistry in a positive way. Pairing that with the healing properties of listening to our favorite music increases our energy, creating an expansive positive energy field, our vibration rises and reaches even further.

Turn up your favorite playlist, grab your pencil and paper, and keep the pencil moving as you dance. It's as if your pencil or paintbrush is your dance partner.

To make things a little easier, attach the paper to your surface with tape, or use an easel that can hold it in place. This way both hands are free. These drawings are not meant to be of anything. The marks are simply a record of our movement. There is so much freedom in putting pencil to paper with no desired or predetermined outcome.

Let go of results and see what happens! This is one of my favorite ways to start a painting! Next time, try it with charcoal, crayon or paint, and notice how different each one feels.

Try the dance party technique to make anything more fun, like laundry! Your raised vibration will act as an invisible shield!

Jessica Lane is a multi-passionate, contemporary artist whose creations inspire others to live their dreams while feeling joy and connection. Being an artist has helped her overcome 25 years of struggling to survive in the deepest depression. Now she celebrates the magic of life and opens doors to new possibilities. Jessica has collectors nationwide, and looks forward to assisting her city with the downtown revamp. Jessica Lane has been featured on www.reddotblog.com, and in Artistonish magazine.

https://www.jmlane.co/

* * *

49

100 paintings in 3 days by Veronica Esqueda

Commit to creating 33 art pieces a day for 3 days (34 on the last day). The idea behind this exercise is to play and be free. When you experiment with this you will discover so much, including: a process (primarily the applied media order), color palette, and textures, to name a few.

When you approach a blank page, you should feel invited, unhindered. I have learned and love so many things about this approach. There are no rules; just be. Immerse yourself and be very present in the process. This can be done at any age. To avoid making a mess or mud, try using only 2-3 colors, not too much water and start slow.

After the three days, I love seeing all of the pieces laid out and I remember each one and the feeling of accomplishment. Personally, this approach helped me get out of my head and just create.

I've also used completed pieces to collage (ripped and pasted to a canvas art piece) and occasionally even unintentionally created small abstracts worthy of gifting or sale.

The Supply list can be basic to unlimited. Simply gathering anything/everything you need from your home, outside, and/or the nearest store. Basically, whatever you find that can make a mark, pattern, or pigment (such as coffee).

Supply List:

Pencils pens markers

Acrylic paints

Acrylic pours

Jar of water for rinsing brushes

Brushes of all sizes and points

Branches (use as a stencil)

Sponges (dab into paint)

Sticks (to make marks into paint)

Tape (lay down before marking)

Leaves

Spray paint / Stencils

Silicone spatulas (for art, sliding paint across the page)

Inks, can be mixed with dabs of water and used as paint

Spray bottle with water for drips

Paint with coffee

Stamps

Kids paint brushes for textures (Sponges and rollers)

Drawing Paper (between 5"x7" and 9"x12")*

If you plan on using wet materials, use mixed media paper.

My name is Veronica M. Esqueda and I am a prophetic mixed media artist. I help those who are in search of meaning in their lives (or perhaps just a little color), to bridge Heaven and Earth by bringing the far things near, so gifts of beauty and light embolden them to embrace the hope and joy that is their legacy.

https://veroarte.co

* * *

50

Connecting with Your Ancestors to Deepen Your Creative Expression by DeVante Love

Before you start creating, be intentional about taking time to connect with your ancestors. Many of us don't remember our childhood or feel disconnected from our past. This results in us feeling separated from a part of ourselves. When we become conscious of this, frustration, doubt, worry, insecurity, and/or fear can creep in and impact our artistic, creative process. These challenging emotional states require specific attention and healing, which, if unresolved, make it hard for us as creators to produce something that represents who we are.

This disconnect from my past made me feel deeply uncomfortable with sharing any of my creations. At that time, I couldn't put my finger on why I disliked my art, writing, and choreography. Everything I innovated lacked the potency I knew it could have. It took me a while to realize that the most potent creations are imbued with a strong sense of identity. The past makes up who we are. Therefore, if we want to create something with that powerful essence that resonates in the world, we must consciously reconnect with our past. Thus the birth of the following ritual practices to reconnect us with our ancestors. Whether alive or transitioned, our ancestors represent all aspects of the past–triumphs, mistakes, hopes, dreams, failures, etc.

As someone who is both African American and Native American, I know my ancestors have endured a lot to create the possibility for my life. Connecting with them does three things.

Firstly, it overwhelms me with gratitude, love, resilience and support–feelings that coincidentally are conducive to creativity. Therefore, each time I connect with my ancestors, I enter into a mental and emotional state where creative energy will likely find me.

Secondly, it creates a sense of expansiveness through my body. Psychologists have already written about how we are more likely to think creatively, critically, or outside of the box when we are relaxed. The practice of connecting with ancestors allows me to access that relaxed, expansive state where all types of creation seem possible.

Thirdly, it takes me away from an egotistical 'me' mindset and nudges me toward a collective 'we' mindset. When creating from this mindset, the impact of our work increases in potency because it now has the potential to resonate more with others.

Here are a couple of easy ritual techniques for connecting with ancestors:
1. Create a small altar positioned next to your desk, easel, mat, writing corner.
2. Light a candle or burn an incense while speaking the name of known ancestors.
3. Say a little prayer to ancestors expressing gratitude for their presence before, during, and/or after creative processes.
4. In moments of freewriting, free drawing, and/or spontaneous movement, invite the ancestors to intervene and guide the moment. Remember to surrender to what comes up rather than immediately judging it or trying

to make sense of it.

5. Listen to music, eat food, adorn yourself with objects that represent your ancestral culture.

DeVante Love (they/them) is a scholar, performer, therapist, and lover of popular culture and spirituality. As one of the few trans monks of color, they are passionate about creating and sharing trauma-informed healing practices that create space for personal liberation. Their passion led them to create Healing Kung Fu—a queer spiritual martial arts academy that holds regular classes and puts on theatrical productions centered around healing. Once they complete their PhD, they plan to continue traveling the world sharing stories and practices of healing.

http://devantelove.com

* * *

51

The Creative Badass by Jo Davis

You read the title and cringed, but don't panic. You are going to be OK. I promise. No grandiose acts of courage are required to get you out of your funk, escape the fun-suck of adulting and take you to that next level of a creative joy-filled life.

Creativity is not some luxury. It is a muscle that we each have. It can restore our sense of wholeness when life goes awry. Tapping into creativity can illuminate our purpose and life path, offering us direction in every area of our life. No massive upheaval of your life is necessary if you stop and listen to the calling NOW. We do this through simple choices, moment to moment, taking small chances, and having the audacity to embrace our inner weird authentic self.

This is the moment you might say, "I'm not a writer, painter, author... I am not a creative person." I would counter that by saying that unless you miraculously came out of the womb, a grown-uptight-40-something, stressed about a mortgage, this is untrue. And, if you are a creative person feeling stuck? This will remind you that you are badass in action. Regardless, there are no accidents. If you are reading this book, I AM TALKING TO YOU.

Creativity is the part of you that is effortless and fluid and goofy. It has no agenda. It does not care what the world thinks. It is play. Pure and simple and courageous. As a five-year-old, you played in the mud, drew on your parents' walls with crayons, and had full-on conversations with your inanimate Barbie or GI Joe's. As children, we spent most of our day living in a make-believe world. That silly space is where ALL things are possible. We are limitless and powerful, during a time when we were still whole and unbroken. We were not control freaks, mending dams, or waiting for the next shoe to drop. We used to be FUN. By reconnecting to this space as an adult, you can free yourself of the opinions of others, release irrational fears and create space for more creativity, intuition and clarity, all while attracting amazing people into your life and developing an epic sense of resilience.

Start here.

• Stop taking yourself so seriously. Find the courage to try something new that is 100% NOT your jam. Laugh at yourself as you fumble. Feel into the ridiculousness of it. Continue doing it until you feel nothing. No embarrassment. Not a care in the world about the outcome of your effort. This could be a new hobby or a class of any kind (art, dance, underwater basket weaving).

• Find courage to be misunderstood. Your need to have control over the outcome of all things and your need to influence how the world sees you is crap. Let it go. Allow the judgment of others to roll off your back.

Start by doing random acts of kindness that make you feel silly. Make it fun! Pass out flowers, love notes, sincere compliments, etc. Expect nothing in return. If people look at you weird? Good! Keep doing it until YOU DON'T CARE WHAT OTHERS THINK.

Be gentle with yourself as you go. Celebrate each little step. Feel the uncomfortableness. Take another step and another.

Get comfortable with looking ridiculous.

Get comfortable with being misunderstood.

Get comfortable with possibly looking like an idiot.

Have fun with it! Involve your most trusted friends in the process! Embrace it. Heck, have a love affair with this newly found habit of COURAGE!

And, for the people watching?

Always! Give them a good show!

Jo Davis is a #1 bestselling author, speaker, gifted intuitive, adventure addict and the Founder of Lift A Sister Up. An organization driven by the belief that our highest calling is to support and inspire other women to chase their dreams both personally and professionally. Jo is a highly gifted intuitive with over 150,000 followers and students. Believing that everyone has these powerful gifts, she shows ordinary people how to tap into their intuitive superpower through her course "Big Mess to Big Magic."

https://liftasisterup.com/

* * *

52

Creativity as a Way of Life by Dawn Dominique

I knew I had to begin my life again but didn't know how to get out of the grips of alcohol. As I traveled down a dangerous and dark path in my addiction, I wanted help so desperately that I finally asked and entered treatment in 2018. Such gratitude for those who helped me on my path of recovery. I was ready and became open, honest and willing to do the inner work necessary to heal and transform my life. Art became a part of that process. It took me a while to see that creativity can truly be a way to see things differently. Being creative is about being curious, resourceful, and up-leveling your imagination. And a mindset to believe in possibilities. Take a class, join a group, and know that whatever you do, it is with an open mind and heart that brings out the beauty, the fun and the joy within all of us.

I was one who believed this crazy statement, "You are not creative as you cannot draw stick figures, paint, or play a musical instrument." Although I tried to play piano a few times and it just drove my brothers to laugh. But what I have found is you don't need those skills to start looking at creativity differently. Think about life hacks that really make things much easier and save time. Think of how movers are able to get so much of your stuff in a medium sized van. They think creatively to stack, figure out the order and make room for everything. There are creative ways of doing, working, believing and seeing things all around us.

I had to learn new ways and design my life differently and would love to share a few ideas to start.

1. Change up your morning routine by having a dance party with your favorite playlist of upbeat songs!

2. Take a different route to wherever you go, change up your meals for the day. I love eating omelets for dinner and dessert for breakfast. For reals. Doing things out of order shifts your energy and elevates your day!

3. Look for classes, group meet ups that bring excitement into your life. Music, art, improv, dance, hiking, building/making something new.

4. Volunteer for anything. Start a walking/running/biking/anything you like group. We are all looking for more connection in our lives and meeting new people with similar interests will bring great energy and enjoyment to your life. I took one art class and felt empowered and energized. And now I paint for fun and relaxation, and use whatever color I feel at the moment. It is amazing what happens when I leave the expectations and outcomes on the floor!

5. Paint an accent wall with your favorite color. Or a whole room. Change the color on your wall once a year.

6. Create a gallery area in your home with inspirational quotes, art, photos, graphics. Start with the largest piece and build around, up, over, and down on the wall of your choice. Pinterest and magazines are my go to for inspiration. And trust your imagination to do the rest.

7. Be in and with nature every chance you can. Allow your senses to come alive! Let your imagination take over as you quiet the mind and feel your way to whatever creative energy shows up. Trust your instincts and intuition to guide you!

8. Start creative gatherings with neighbors/friends by setting out a table

with a colored tablecloth and ask everyone to bring a couple of art supplies. Create a theme of the month - Adult finger-painting is a blast! A collaborative collage is fun too!

All these ways have given me healing, hope and inspiration to live happy, joyous and free one day at a time. Creativity is my way of life now. Take the chance and do something new and know the possibilities exist for all of us in the unlimited opportunities to awaken our creative spirit.

Dawn Dominique is a joy seeker, creativity facilitator, author, and a self taught intuitive artist who enjoys bright and bold colors in her mixed media and large canvas paintings. She believes that everyone is creative because we are alive! Dawn lives in the beautiful Blue Ridge mountains in western North Carolina where waterfalls, lush forests and hiking are a way of life. She is a fur baby mom to two fun and feisty kitty's and loves the white squirrels that show up often in her backyard. Dawn is following her calling where she guides people to awaken to their own creative spirit and to live a life with curiosity, wonder, and joy!

She brings together people for creative adventures where nature, art and fun gatherings can include attending live music and theater performances, visiting fun and eclectic art galleries, open studio tours, and creative circles to work on projects and share ideas with like minded people. Dawn loves to build community and connection through her intuitive creativity workshops that bring an energy and enthusiasm from the very start. It takes courage, a curious heart, and willingness to begin your own adventure in designing a life that is authentically creative.

http://www.awakeningyourcreativity.com

* * *

53

Choose a Specific Time Each Day and Just Begin! by Debbie Viola

As the years turned into decades, I grew more dissatisfied with my New York City corporate job. I was trading way too much time for way too little money, and felt like my family life was being sacrificed. Arriving home in a cab after my kids were already asleep was a far too common occurrence. The occasional meager bonus served as a small reward, but deep down I felt like I was wishing my life away, waiting for the weekends so I could be with my husband and two kids. Despite feeling this way, I continued to live a robotic, dutiful life to provide for my family. I gained instant clarity the moment my boss of 23 years asked me to take work with me because I was 'leaving early'. It wouldn't be the first time I took work with me when working 8 or 9 hours in the office wasn't enough for him.

But this time it was different—it was September 11, 2001, and it was about 11:00 in the morning. When those words came out of his mouth, it sickened me that work was still the only thing on his mind, especially since he was just screaming that his close friend was at a meeting in one of the Towers. Right then and there, I knew with certainty that I never wanted to work for anyone but myself ever again as long as I could help it. I just knew in my gut that I didn't want another 20+ years to go by, and regret that I never took the chance to change my life. If I didn't make the bold move then, I knew I never would. Despite not having a plan, I made the bold decision to chuck in the steady paycheck, pursue my newfound hobby of decorative painting, and figure out how to make a living from it. I didn't even know what an entrepreneur was, but suddenly I was one.

Twenty-two years later, and I still pinch myself that I was brave enough to break free and change the trajectory of my life in ways I never could have imagined. I get to do what I love and make people happy. I've been voted Best Artist of Long Island, NY several years in a row, have been on four TV shows and several podcasts, and a NY publisher wants me to write a book to "inspire women all over the world."But the most gratifying of all is that I get to share my talent with my clients by creating art to enhance their homes and businesses, while teaching others how to get started in their creative journey.

We live in an uncertain stressful world, and it's important more than ever to indulge in a creative hobby to give your brain a mental rest. My first suggestion for bringing more creativity into your life is to set aside a specific time each day. This will help you to become more consistent and form a habit. I am a night owl, and I love painting at midnight when the house is quiet and without interruptions. If you don't know how to get started, neither did I. I know I'm aging myself, but back then, there was no Internet! I had to go to the library and find books on how to get started painting in acrylics. So I've become passionate about explaining things in simple language that anyone can understand.

My goal is to take away the frustration and make it nice and easy so there's no question on how to begin. The cost of art supplies can run the gamut, but you shouldn't let that stop you. Post-pandemic, you can now go into your local dollar store and find paintbrushes, surfaces, and acrylic paint. As far as colors go, red, blue, yellow, white and black are all you need. All the other fancy stuff associated with being an artist is optional. You can just start with those basics, some paper towels, a water cup, and add on as you become more comfortable. If you don't have a designated space, get a plastic container to put your supplies in so they can easily be moved from room to room.

I've taught thousands of students of all ages, both locally and online, and I let them in on my little secret—a roll of wax paper is your best friend.

1. Lay down two large pieces of wax paper in front of you; use the top piece to mix and blend your colors.
2. Dip your brush into a color, and blend the brush back and forth on the wax paper, so that the paint evenly moves up into the bristles, or else you'll have a blob of paint. You also can use its slick surface to practice a stroke over and over, or you can create a whole painting right on the wax paper.
3. Play around by mixing two colors, and you'll be amazed at all the different colors you can create. My students have dubbed me "Debbie Dabber," because I teach how to dab the paintbrush onto the surface, one color at a time, for a beautiful landscape, even if you're a beginner.
4. As you become more daring, you can paint a little design in the corner of any outgoing mail. I'm sure my bill collectors loved receiving roses on their envelopes in the mail. Once you start looking around your house, you'll be surprised at what you'll find to practice on.

As your skills improve, you'll surely want to play around with different surfaces, and you might find yourself running out of space. I've proven myself as an artist, because now I have a dedicated home studio that's my favorite place in the world to be.

Debbie Viola is a fine abstract artist whose intuitive paintings are a natural extension of being a fine finish painter and surface designer for the past 22 years. Picking up a paintbrush for the first time in 1998 at age 40, Debbie embraces the adage, 'it's never too late'. Debbie runs a multi-faceted decorative arts studio, having done restoration work for Ritz-Carlton Central Park and Saint Agnes Cathedral. Her solo art exhibit showcasing over 40 large paintings, was broadcast on Fios1 News during its gala opening. She was featured on the cover of Sunday Newsday, one of the top ten U.S. newspapers, has appeared on five podcasts, was named "Extraordinary Woman of Nassau County," and has been voted Best Artist of Long Island, New York several years in a row. Debbie has appeared on ABC, CBS (twice) and NBC (twice).
http://www.debbieviolafineart.com

Visit https://bit.ly/3ihYmbi and click on the "Free Art" button to download and enjoy my popular painting, "Peaceful".

54

Dive In! by Jenny Hull

You ARE creative!

We are all born with an instinctive desire to create. After all, we are created in the image of THE original Creator. The ability to create is there the moment we are born. Each of us possesses gifts and talents that are uniquely our own. Before us, an exciting journey of discovering our creative bent awaits.

Have you ever seen something made by an artisan and thought, "Wow, that's so beautiful, I wish I could do that?" I say you CAN! Every one of you reading this has the capacity to explore and discover what gifts you have. To fulfill that desire to create something inspired and imaginative.

While we are very young, we're encouraged to explore our artistic abilities. Crayons, Play-Doh, clay and paints are some of the tools we learn to use. There are lots of toys that encourage us to use our hands in a way that teaches creative skills.

Too often along the way, the potential for discovering how artistic or creative we are is stifled. The teacher, who thought they were helping you when they told your five year old self, "try coloring the tree green instead of purple," caused you to pull back on your creative expression. The time someone told you your drawing didn't look real enough, you began to believe that though you loved drawing, you couldn't do it. When someone laughed at what you created and you allowed what others thought to hinder your artistic expression. This may be you, but don't let that hold you back.

My creativity hack is simple. Dive in! If it appeals to you, try it. Jump in with no expectations other than to enjoy the exploration. Creativeness dwells inside every aspect of life. I'll give you a list of suggestions to begin to explore. I hope you add many more yourself.

- Treat each experience as if it were a spa day. Savor your new experiences and find the thing that lights a spark within you.
- Try poetry or writing that novel.
- Buy a nice notebook and a fancy pen.
- Light a scented candle and play soft music and let the prose flow.
- Take a fancy cooking class with a friend.
- Sign up for pottery classes with your significant other.
- Buy some paint, brushes (fingers work too!) and paper or canvas.
- Watch a YouTube tutorial and have fun!
- Buy a calligraphy pen and how-to book, or watch some YouTube tutorials.
- Buy some chalk and a chalk board and play with creating fancy chalkboard art.
- Buy a needle felting, cross stitch, needlepoint or quilt applique kit. They come with all the needed items to complete a project.
- Treat yourself to your favorite movie while stitching.
- Teach yourself to knit or crochet using a how-to book or video.
- Practice taking imaginative photographs and videos.
- Learn to play an instrument.
- Write a song.
- Find some plans on Pinterest and build a new side table for your living room.

- Write a children's book.
- If you have young children don't forget to include them as well. They love to explore and learn and will benefit for a lifetime with your encouragement. There is nothing quite so freeing as finger painting.

So go ahead and have fun exploring your creativity. Remember, instead of wishing you could, say to yourself, "I'm learning to make that." Who knows what incredible things you will create. Share with me how you have found your creative path, and let's inspire each other!

Jenny Hull is an artist who enjoys helping people discover their own creativity. She helps them to fulfill their desire of crafting something unique with their own hands. Jenny is the owner of Jenny Hull Studios where she creates and sells art. A wife of 38 years and mother of 3 girls she has explored many avenues of creativity throughout the years. From textiles to photography to fine art she is happy to share her knowledge with others. Featured in the online magazine Voyage Savannah, Jenny is looking forward to more media opportunities in 2023.

https://www.instagram.com/jennyhullstudios/

* * *

55

Art and Creativity to Free your Unconscious Mind by Nishah Dennison

reativity and art activate a state of healing. The creative process itself, allows your true and authentic self to be freely expressed.

Our Creative State can be described as:

- Organic (from within)
- Spontaneous (no censorship)
- In the Moment (out of our heads)

When you create, know that whatever needs expressing will be expressed, negative as well as positive. See creativity as a release.

Below is my Triple Gem Method:

GEM 1: Use Art/Creativity in Place of Meditation

Not all of us are good at meditating—by this I mean sitting still and watching the breath; so, having a specific focus, that is a repetitive non-thinking activity is extremely helpful.

Use art, or another creative activity to switch off. Turn to meditative art/creation when feeling unclear or out of sorts. You may find yourself suddenly freed-up afterwards.

GEM 2: Use Art/Creativity to Balance and Release

If your mind is disturbed—Depressed, Anxious, Low Esteem, Existential crisis—get creative! Creativity will allow you to off load, expel and release. Do not be afraid to create something 'dark'—this is called releasing your 'shadow'. We want this to be out, rather than held in.

The results can be further processed (What does this say about me? Do I need to do anything with this?) or simply seen as released and gone. No action required.

GEM 3: Use Art/Creativity to Express Your Authentic Self

Satisfy an urge to be yourself by putting an image to your thoughts, thinking or feeling. See this as bringing something to the surface to be born! This creative expression firms up a sense of self and makes us feel more whole.

What do you have the urge to create? Don't censor, be spontaneous.

How big will this be? What materials feel right? Which colours are essential? It's exciting and thrilling to be YOU!

REMEMBER!—Being Creative and Expressing Creativity is both Healthy and Healing.

Nishah Dennison is an expert in helping people leverage their powerful and creative unconscious mind, so they can master their lives with mental resilience, deep inner security and a purposeful sense of freedom.

Nishah is a published and exhibited artist, holding multiple art qualifications and has trained in Cambridge, London and Bangkok. She also holds multiple advanced qualifications in psychotherapy, working as a therapist for nearly three decades. She combines psychotherapy and spirituality into her art. Her multifaceted career history includes NHS Public Health Advising, Professional Burnout Debriefing, Tate Gallery Exhibitions Manager, Director and Professor of Psychotherapy Training at Regents University, and more.

Nishah describes her early life as 'living blindly', therefore her passion is for people to have a robust life strategy with vision and clarity, be armed with psychological and creative tools, and fully embrace their dreams with joyous living.

She is a master of Dream Analysis and an advocate of Art and Creativity as essential to healthy living. The multiple arms of her brand ignite, impact and inspire rapid growth, through her method of dynamic psychoeducation, consultancy, speaking and writing. Some of her interviews are listed below:

How I reinvented myself in the second chapter of my life; Creating a ripple effect by cultivating joy; How we can optimize our mental, physical, emotional and spiritual wellbeing.

https://www.facebook.com/nishah.dennison

* * *

56

Change Your Mindset and Manifest Your Dreams by Deanna Aliano

I found my passion later in life and became an artist. This experience changed me forever. It taught me to take the chance when I feel that something is right. There is a lot of information out there about believing in your passion and how to manifest, but removing our traumas and negative beliefs is the first step to manifestation. When we are trapped and influenced by incorrect and unhelpful beliefs without realizing it, we lack the clarity to know what we need and the ability to manifest it. Or, we continually manifest things that are not what we say we want because the negative programming is always running in the background of our brain without us realizing it.

So, the first step is to consider where in life you have reached the wrong conclusion about a subject that is now a part of your world view. This "head trash" just needs to be discovered and removed for your dreams to have a chance. For many people, as an example, beliefs around money are preventing them from manifesting money into their lives.

The most important part of manifesting is to listen to how you feel when you are making decisions in life. Do you feel frightened, desperate or feeling down? This is not the time to move forward.

According to the National Science Foundation, "an average person has about 12,000 to 60,000 thoughts per day. Of those, 80% are negative and 95% are repetitive thoughts." A powerful hack is to grab a pen and paper and write down unhelpful thoughts that are in your head as they occur. "There's never enough time, money doesn't grow on trees, I can't get anything right, Mondays suck" or whatever. Then, for every negative thought, write at least one better thought. This is called a reframe. Cognitive reframing is a technique used to shift your mindset so you're able to look at a situation, person, or relationship from a slightly different perspective.

What do you do with trash? Throw it out. When your mind falsely says to you something like "everything is horrible," "you're a terrible friend," "This will never work" etc? Head trash! Sometimes even just saying that phrase makes me laugh and helps me realize my brain is trying to trick me into believing nonsense to stop myself from changing or achieving a new goal.

The next step after becoming aware and keeping track of unhelpful thoughts is to take the time to step back and do something you enjoy. Laugh with a friend, exercise, paint if you are an artist, or spend time with children, experiment with the thing that scares you and actually do it, even if it's a baby step. When you are feeling happy and energized is the best time to take action. This has worked for me so many times and has taught me to let go of the outcome and fears about the outcome, not just when I am painting, but in my life, while simply staying with the feeling of joy and trusting the process without attachment.

I trust in myself and the universe to bring me everything I need. We have been taught to play it safe and if we want more out of life we have to jump in and make it happen. When the opportunity comes, take it! I spend more time trusting my intuition. This practice has guided me to so many opportunities in the last two years. I purchased a condo on the beach with so many obstacles that many would think it would never happen. I always dreamed of living near the ocean. I also started my Art Business and I'm building confidence every day. I have invested in myself and my love for art.

I wish for you to follow your passion and manifest your dreams!

Deanna is a Florida abstract and landscape artist. She is a self-taught artist who found her love for painting 6 years ago. Her paintings are created with many different types of paint and mediums. Acrylic, watercolor, and various types of inks. She is known for using vibrant colors and loves trying new techniques.

https://prints.artbydeanna.com

* * *

57

Romanticize Your Life...The Art of Expressive Living by Caroline Karp

A s an artist, the art of expressive living is all about living a life full of creativity, spontaneity, and joy. It means infusing every moment of our lives with a sense of wonder and magic and embracing every opportunity to explore our creative potential.

One hack to bring this art into our lives is to create a daily ritual of movement and creativity.

1. Start your day by moving your body out in nature, whether it's taking a walk or doing yoga.
2. Then, paint from your heart and soul every day, even if it's just for a few minutes.
3. Incorporate play into your life by riding your bike along the water, playing pickleball, or spending time with children.
4. Approach tasks with a childlike wonder and curiosity, and seek out new experiences that ignite your sense of adventure.
5. Connect with other artists and collectors around the world by jumping in and founding an online art collective.

6. Host a podcast about artists' inspirations and connect more deeply with your community.
7. Write and illustrate a series of children's books about expressive living through the eyes of a child.
8. Take your art to the streets by going out and painting live in big cities and by the ocean.
9. Travel to new places to seek inspiration and capture the beauty of the world through your art.
10. Finally, nourish your body and soul by eating healthy food, laughing, singing, and dancing.

When you embrace the art of expressive living, every moment becomes an opportunity to create, explore, and experience the magic of life.

Everyone has talent. The secret is how you use it.

If you do not feel up to the challenge… work with a master artist to guide you through the amazing process of how to flow. Lean into the support, open up to possibilities, loosen up, tune into intuition, release expectations, and welcome joyful, authentic expression and creativity.

Witness your fantastic new way of living unfold.

Caroline Karp is a world-renowned multi-talented artist, author, illustrator, educator, and podcaster, known for her romantic expressionistic paintings of iconic buildings, sailboats and sunflowers. Her passion for art has led her to travel and establish studios in Washington D.C., Kauai, and Tampa Bay. Caroline's art captures the essence of the environment, embodying the energy of expression in her work. As a Plein Air painter, Caroline uses an expressionistic perspective to capture moments and places. Her paintings are known for their boldness and the intense emotion that comes with the creation process. Her work has been commissioned by people around the world, including celebrities. In her workshops and retreats, she helps women learn to live expressively. Her dedication to the well-being of humankind and her belief in the power of art to inspire, provoke, and heal make Caroline Karp a true inspiration in the world of art. Caroline has been recognized as an international artist and has been featured in several podcasts and publications, such as New Visionary, The Georgetowner, and Art NXT Level. Caroline is also the founder of the International Online Art Collective, a group of artists from around the world coming together to share art from their studios to the globe. As a live painter, Caroline creates a sacred space where she can share her heart, be authentic, and allow creativity to flow. She is dedicated to the well-being of humankind and believes that making art is a journey into the unknown, an awakening of the heart. With her unique combination of talents, Caroline Karp is a true inspiration in the world of art. Caroline obtained her BFA from Florida State University in 1991 and her MA from the University of Colorado. Upon graduating, she moved to Colorado for ten years to continue her career as a painter and educator. After living in Denver, she is now living in Clearwater, Florida where you can find her on the golf course, pickleball court, out on the water or in her studio painting.

https://www.carolinekarpartist.com/

* * *

58

Seeing Like an Artist by Carol MacConnell

I still remember the first day I could see like an artist. I was driving in my car, looking out the window, and the magic happened. The world opened up. I could see shapes and colors that before were grass and houses. I could see the negative shapes between the branches of the trees. I felt like the colors were electric.

I started out as a classically trained realistic painter. When you're a realistic artist, it's all about measuring. I'm going to show you how to see as an artist through measuring. All you need is a pencil, a piece of paper, and your hands.

Place your hand, palm up, on the table. What do you see? You probably see your palm, your thumb, and four fingers. If you went to draw it, you would probably name each item as you attempt to draw them. "Here's my little finger, and my ring finger, and my middle finger, and so forth." Try it and see what you draw.

Now let me tell you what I see as an artist. I see the space between the thumb and the pointer finger. I see the shape of the line from my wrist to the end of my thumb. I see the "bumps" in the line as I follow it to the end of my fingernail. I see the three totally different shapes that are formed between each of my fingers. I see the line from my wrist to the tip of my baby finger and how much it is different from the one to the tip of my thumb. I see the width of my palm compared to the width of each finger.

Once you open your mind to seeing things like an artist, you will open up a whole new view of your world. Everything you look at, you'll find yourself saying. "Now how would I paint that?" What would I leave out? What would I emphasize? How could I simplify what was in front of me? What shapes do I see? What's in the light? What's in the shadow? Your view of the world will shift, and a new way of seeing will evolve.

By the way, did you know that your hand is the same size as your face? Put the base of your hand right above the wrist, at the bottom of your face, and extend your fingers.

Amazing, Isn't it?

I'm always painting with my eyes, even when I'm not painting.

Carol MacConnell is a versatile and prolific contemporary artist who creates painting solutions for interior designers and corporate clients. She also works with couples and individuals to select the perfect piece of art for their homes. With a

Fine Arts degree, Carol worked many years in the corporate sector before taking the leap into running her own art business. She now has a studio/gallery and an ecommerce website from which she sells her art. Carol also has more than 10,000 followers on Instagram, where she posts daily.

https://www.carolmacconnell.com/

* * *

59

Showing Up Is Your First Creative Act by Michaelene Shannon

Once you've shown up, the rest will fall into place as you recognize that your most significant masterpiece is you. Intentional creativity is about making the greatest promise to yourself and then sharing the whole you with the world. Everyone has an ability to express themselves in a number of ways and creating art is your unique gift of expression. There is no other you and your creations represent authentic expression. When you show up for yourself in this way, the benefits will amaze you and expand your life beyond limitation. Creating not only opens the doors of possibility, it activates your senses to previously unknown levels of energy and vibrancy. To show up and create is your birthright!

Windows of Perception In 7 easy steps.

This creative activity will provide you with lots of enjoyment now and in the future. Whilst creating, you can listen to music and allow your body to move—you are flowing with creativity. From the wellspring of your intention and your movement, a new experience is released, energy is expressed vibrantly, your mind begins to shift into a state of receptivity and the creative pathway is open and flowing. By its very nature, creativity spills out into other areas of your life.

1. Give Yourself Permission to Play!
2. Gather Materials: paper (I use large sheets of watercolour paper or from a mixed media book), mark making tools (acrylic paint, acrylic ink, pens, markers, pencils, crayons), painter's tape, ruler, and scissors (optional). If you opt for painting, you will need at least one paintbrush, acrylic paint, and a jar of water to clean the brushes. You can use all of the mark making tools listed above or stay with one kind; for example, use only paint or just pens. You don't need to have oodles of supplies to begin, although heavier paper is best. What you have is enough—you are enough!
3. Begin: by placing your paper on a smooth, firm surface such as a table
4. Tape: your paper in equidistant sections using a ruler to measure for accuracy. Depending on the size of your paper, you might have as few as 2 or as many as 12 'windows' (squares or rectangles) of the same size. Extend each strip of tape beyond the page onto the table and your paper will be well secured.
5. Choose: your 'tool' of choice (pen, paintbrush, etc.). What colour are you drawn to? Pick that one to start with. Now, using that tool mark the page on all or only some of the windows. Vary the mark on each—a swooping motion can be liberating and exciting. Or, use more deliberate marks; the idea is to explore and have fun. Choose another tool or another colour and put down more marks. This activity lends itself well to abstract design. Set your worry mind at ease—this is not about perfection.
6. Step: back or to the side and look at your paper. What other colour, shape or thickness of line do you want to add?
7. Continue: until you feel a sense of completion and once it is dry, remove the tape and voila, you have a visual document of your personal 'Windows of Perception'

NOW WHAT TO DO WITH YOUR CREATION?

- Leave the entire page whole & adhere to a wall as though you were looking through a multi-paned window—Smile each time you pass by it.
- Cut your 'windows' evenly and post them around the house.
- Write something inspiring in the white space under each art window.
- Sign your art windows.
- Frame your art squares.
- Gift them to others with a personalized note written in the white space or on the back.
- Share them as 'love notes' on special occasions to those you care about.
- Tuck them randomly into books (like How To or cookbooks) so that you will be surprised and delighted by one of your windows when you least expect it.

What ideas do you have for your windows?

Congratulations, You Fabulous Creative Being. Keep showing up for your creative practice—you are worth it! Explore other creative activities and expand even more. Hey, develop one of your own creativity hacks!

Michaelene is committed to conscious creativity as a regular life practice which includes painting, writing, photography and dancing. As a self-taught artist along

with doing a few workshops, being in Nature is a guiding force in her creative adventures. Her poems have been published in an e-chapbook titled Water and was shortlisted in the 2023 Scugog Arts Literary Contest. She shares her passion with others and offers coaching in the hopes that they too will tap into their own creative source. Allowing yourself to be intentionally creative will help you live your best life!

https://www.instagram.com/michaeleneshannonart/

* * *

60

Poem "Pilots Belong in the Sky" Can Inspire Hope by Wendy Drews

If you think about giving up, just think of the sky—how beautiful it is and how everyday it's never the same. It's constantly changing and that's how life is. You can have a bad day and be so hopeless but the next day is nothing but blue skies. So if you're feeling like you're going to give up, think of the sky.

S-Somebody K-Knows Y-You.

My Creative Hack is that Art can Heal.

There is more than higher education or college which didn't lead the way for my healing. You can choose more than one form of art medium. I chose Photography, Writing, Ceramics, Sculpture, and Painting.

Let your heart guide you to the performance art of oneself. I knew that by picking up a camera that it would lead me the way back to myself. To know yourself is to really heal yourself.

I have always had a connection with water. Being in water or near water is very healing for my mind, body, and soul. I have always loved waterfalls, sunsets, and the sky. I feel a sense of serenity when incorporating imagery of what I love. I feel these are the miracles of our world and I am drawn to the elements of nature.

Photography makes us feel emotions when capturing a piece of time. Memories are forever preserved in our hearts as sometimes the mind can forget moments of time.

Enrich your mind but always follow your heart. I, as an artist, hope to inspire others to follow what they love for inner wisdom, peace, and healing.

Remember S.K.Y. can be a sense of calm for others during turbulent times. Being outdoors with nature, wildlife, waterfalls, the sea, sunsets, and the sky has left a great impression on me.

Art can heal people.

Becoming a creative person can really pave the way to becoming self-sufficient.

Start with yourself and find your own personal statement. Take the time to know who you really are and become your own hero. Then connect with a community and become part of something bigger than yourself. Once you are a part of a thriving creative community your outreach to help people is endless. That's when creativity can build that life that you don't need to heal from. Don't be afraid to invest in oneself and find connections.

We are constantly evolving, growing, and experiencing life that there is so much to offer our loved ones, communities, and the entire world.

My creative ideas are to help people step into who they are no matter what. Truth, honor, dignity, respect, and having a strong self love is important to find out who you are.

My poem Pilots Belong in the Sky can inspire hope. We are all rising butterflies ready to thrive and change the world. We have the choice to heal and become our own hero and Fly Dream Remember Sky.

Wendy Drews is a professional visual artist and writer, working at the intersection of math, science, photography, and art. She came up with the acronym SKY—Somebody Knows You. She created this to inspire people not to give up hope.

www.skyseawolfstudios.com

* * *

61

Time Travel to Childhood by Zya Be

When we are children, the world is filled with possibility. We leap into every moment, and find joy everywhere. We explore our world with wonder and play with enthusiasm. These qualities, which are instinctive to children, are at the heart of what it means to be creative.

As we grow up, we are told the 'right way' to do things: color inside the lines, follow rules, focus on success. We then become worried about what others think, afraid of making mistakes and ultimately, we tend to lose touch with our youthful characteristics. Our lives can feel flat and uninspiring, leaving us wanting more.

What if we could reclaim our childhood qualities? Good news—we can! And it will not only enhance your creativity, it will also vastly improve almost every area of your life. Happier relationships with more play? Oh yes! Better solutions with more curiosity? You bet!

Let's start and rev up your creative fire!

Get out of your mind and into your body—It may not be easy for you to shift from hectic, stressful days to simply sit down to paint or sing. To really tap into your authentic expression, you will want to get out of your logical thinking mind and reconnect with your body where you can create with flow and ease. For example, when you are dancing with abandon, are you planning how your arm will move next or do you just let your body do its thing?

Our wise young creativity mentors, children, act without thought or reason. They do not plan or analyze what to do; they just let their body move. They pretend they are animals, jump on their beds, splash in the bath. Once you are connected with your body, you will be able to more easily express your creativity fully.

Practice Zone: Here are a few fast, easy methods to quiet your thinking mind and reconnect with your body: meditate, sing along to your favorite music, savor a tasty treat, laugh out loud about nothing, move your body—dance, stretch, do yoga, go for a walk, shake your body.

Now that your body is buzzing with excitement, let's move on to children's next lesson for creativity.

Enjoy the experience—Young children do not worry about the end result of what they are doing or judge their effort; they are too busy having fun. Look at my bio photo—It is clear that I thought that smearing paint everywhere was an amazing activity. I had no thought of whether my art was 'good', how it 'should' look or how it compared to others' creations.

Give yourself permission to simply enjoy the creative process. There are no mistakes in this approach. Everything is an exploration, an experience simply for the joy of that moment. Be amazed with yourself and what you create. When you let go of the end point, you free yourself and open to new possibilities and surprises.

Practice Zone: Plan to throw away your creation when it is done so there is no attachment to it. Keep no record of it. Knowing the art will be destroyed allows you to experiment. You do not need to be precious with materials, careful with your brushstrokes, intentional with your color combinations or purposeful with your composition. None of that matters. Also, as you are creating, catch your inner critic and tell it that you do not need its opinion; you are enjoying yourself.

Obviously, you will not always want to discard your work. This is a suggestion to shift to non-judgmental, fully-engaged creation. It can be done at the start of a creating session as a refresher or anytime you catch yourself getting too serious or critical of yourself and your work.

Be Curious—Kids ask questions, they investigate and love to learn. Over time, many of us lose that sense of curiosity. We stop exploring, we worry about how someone will view us for asking questions or we think we already have the answers.

To get your curiosity and sense of wonder back, approach every situation with an open mind, consider different viewpoints (even literally—laying down or standing on a chair can help), and be willing to learn and try new methods and activities.

Practice Zone: 'What if' is great to spark creativity and bring new energy to your expression.

Here are a few sample prompts to bring curiosity to your creative pursuits: What if I use crayon over paint? What if I only use my non-dominant hand? What if I dance using only my upper body? What if I write only in 4-word sentences? What if I sing a different style? What if I sculpted a moving cloud?

What 'what ifs' can you come up with?

Play—Kids love to play. It is how they learn about the world and develop their imaginations. As we grow up, we tend to take life more seriously. We forget about the importance of play and start to see it as a waste of time. Let go and have fun—your inner child will thank you for it!

Practice Zone: Again, these are initial ideas. Simply pondering unique ways to play will get your creative juices flowing. Watch kids for extra inspiration.

Paint play—splash, splatter, pour, drip. Paper play—roll, cut, rip, crumple, fold, glue. Drawing play—draw holding a crayon between your teeth or your toes. Musical play—create comical song lyrics or make up a new language and sing the national anthem for your imaginary country (These 2 are fabulous when stuck in traffic or even just at a red light.)

Create smiles with food in your meals. Make funny faces as you create. Give yourself challenges such as making a colorful necklace from materials in your kitchen.

Be ridiculous. Laugh!

There you have it—the four qualities of a young child that can help you boost your creativity and create your '**hell yes**' life: **get into your body, enjoy the experience, be curious** and **play**! Embrace these ways of living and see where they take you—you might be surprised at the magic that unfolds!

Note: Practice zone examples can be used as warm ups to any creative pursuit or used on their own to nurture your inner artist.

Zya Be is committed to igniting a global movement of women trailblazing their 'hell yes' lives that light them up and inspire those around them to do the same.

Zya has been crafting her own unique path most of her adult life. After 10 years in corporate America climbing the ladder, she broke free. At 29, she took a year-long sabbatical to travel the world solo. In the years to come, Zya continued to explore, reaching every continent solo by 39. Between trips, she built a multi-million dollar organizational change consulting firm that led transformation for Fortune 500 companies. In 2019, she retired from consulting and closed her firm.

Since then, Zya funneled her lifelong desire to support women, decades of expertise in guiding change and signature sass into Your Hell Yes Life. She is in the beginning stages of this exciting adventure. Your Hell Yes Life will be a place of growth, community and celebration where every woman is inspired to take bold action and slash expectations to experience massive joy and live however the hell they want.

Random facts—Zya will break into dance anywhere, paints bold colorful abstract images and is immensely grateful that her parents supported her creativity from the very beginning.

https://www.instagram.com/yourhellyeslife

* * *

62

Be Creative with Frequency Music and Spreadsheets by Veronique Marchal

Being asked for my "creative hacks" to share with you, I have chosen my top 3 that bring the best in me alive these days: Environment and ambiance set the tone, and creativity with words can open up our hearts and minds

So, what are you looking at? Smelling? I like incense and/or a candle.

1) Listening to? My go to more and more is "frequency music," by Barry Goldstein, "Secret Language of the Heart." I especially listen to it when "on my laptop"—reading, responding to emails, and definitely when writing a larger communication or creative conceptualization in Canva, for social media or a website. I am designing my own music DJ lists to ground or power up! Frequency music while flying in a plane, and driving home—wow!

2) As I read, I highlight and take notes in the margins or in a notebook that later get transferred to a spreadsheet (like a table or chart). Yes, I said spreadsheet (Nod of appreciation to the retired Navy SEAL sniper instructor who introduced spreadsheets and their purpose into my life). How un-artistic, right? Yes, and... As it turns out, "they" open up the possibility of

231

holding and capturing one or two (cells of notes/words) at a time and placing them in a new "document." I like adding other elements and words that seem to emerge during the moments when I am bringing together different sources—maybe a particular bird outside my window? An object in the room seems to want me to notice it, its purpose, its message.

This practice has recently helped me creatively express my grief and disbelief about people, practices and the planet that matter to me and to "we." For example, an "animal spirit card" from Colette Baron-Reid "appeared" in the form of an "ant" as I was alchemizing and "word-dancing" with Caste by Isabel Wilkerson and a few other books—reminding me of the power of collaboration and community.

These practices are part of my (in-design and development) creative "we-me books,""We Me Inspire Action Kit,"Happy Hours, Power Hours and Actionshop innovations. You, friends, co-workers and family are invited to add your "me" to our "we!"

3) My mind and eyes see a "word inside a word" or a slight "rewording" that gives deeper and expanded meanings and possibilities, such as the letter "W":

"W" if flipped upside down or reflected, it becomes "M"

So that

WE becomes ME

EMPOWER becomes WEPOWER and/or MEPOWER

Shall we dance?

I was born in France and French was my first language. We moved to the USA before I could walk or talk—giving me a deep appreciation for "me" and "we" at all times.

You're invited to grow with me. My Life's Creative Expression: We Me Planet and We Me People. https://linktr.ee/wemeaction

Over the last two decades I have explored many nonviolent, compassion-contemplative and life performance practices not only to become a better version of my Self, but to also be of my utmost service to People and Planet. Today, I am a happier and healthier version of my Self when I create practices and environments that bring out the creative Artist in my heart and mind.

Professionally, I have always worked with some form of communications, public relations/media relations, corporate sponsorship, community engagement or fundraising roles. From five-star hotels, VIP credentials, press conferences and private security guards to prisons to clambakes to Save a River... "it" has been an epic journey so far, and only getting more creative and enjoyable!

At my core and at my whisper of my Self, I am an Artist—and profoundly believe that we all are Artists! Creativity is our human super power! I have never really led or been paid for offering traditional works of art (painting, photography, singing, dancing, writing, acting, sculpturing, etc). I love to dance—anyone who knows me knows this to be true! With dance, I have found a more powerful and personal "happening." When I dance or move to music without words or lyrics and, ideally with a song that I have never heard before it really brings me into the moment and my body fully! This "newness" allows for whatever emotion or speed or lightness of movement to arise as the notes and melody dance with me in the moment. This allowing and experiencing the unknown, unchoreographed and improvised stays with me as I get older more deeply and lastingly "dancing with me" as I bring together different words written by different authors and sources in order to create an alchemy of "words dancing together" because if they (the words) were human, I believe they would want to "dance together"—or at least try to—with some "words" leading some days, other sources another, in lock-step chorus line, two-stepping, swaying, waltzing, tangoing, breaking, salsa-ing and of course, improvising!

https://linktr.ee/wemeaction

* * *

63

My Daily Art Journal Practice by Christy Kale

I've been an artist for most of my adult life. Painting is one of the most joyful parts of my creative journey. However, over the years I have experienced periods of "artist's block" that have prevented me from creating for months at a time. For me, this type of creative block can be emotionally quite painful, frustrating, and paralyzing. I have found that a simple daily art journal practice keeps me "in flow" with and connected to my creativity.

Doing this quick and simple daily practice has had a profound effect on my ability to pick up a paint brush and get to work easily and quickly, without all the feelings of creative block and procrastination that plagued me for years. By using this journal, I've discovered that my art is improving even when I'm not in the studio!

Each morning I open my art journal. On the left-hand side I put down a layer of acrylic paint, choosing the color of the paint based on how I'm feeling that day. Throughout the day I return to the journal and add paint, marks, or scribbles to the artwork. By the end of the day, I have a small painting or drawing to remember how I'm feeling that day.

My goal here is simple artistic expression and practice, not a finished work of art. This practice can be incredibly freeing and lead to unexpected surprises or "happy accidents" I can then use in my studio work.

On the right-hand side of the journal, I write the date at the top of the page and make notes about ideas I have for future work, what I did that day, ideas for titles for my paintings, things I want to remember to do, and really anything I want to keep track of as the day goes on.

For this project you can use any kind of journal or sketchbook you like. I recommend a 5" x 8" or 6" x 9" journal or sketchbook. I prefer a journal I can fit into the small backpack I use as a purse. Sometimes I use a 5.5" x 8.5" art sketchbook with heavyweight watercolor paper (270 gsm weight paper with 104 unnumbered pages). If I want a journal with more pages, I will use a medium A5 (5-3/4" x 8-1/4") dotted bullet journal with lighter weight paper (120 gsm weight paper and 204 numbered pages). Once you coat the lighter weight paper with gesso or acrylic paint, the paper becomes thicker and can hold the weight of the paint.

What art supplies are needed? You can use any type of art supplies in your art journal, from pens, pencils, colored pencils, crayons, markers, felt pens, watercolor, collage, cut paper, to acrylic or gouache paint. My favorite art supplies are acrylic and gouache paints, crayons (I like Caran d'Ache Neocolor II pastels), pencils and graphite sticks, and markers (Posca are my favorite). If I want to take my art journal on the road with me, I create a small travel pack of art supplies with felt pens, pencils, a pencil sharpener, markers, brushes, and small bottles or tubes of acrylic or gouache paint. I put them in a cigar box or a flat plastic Tupperware container and off I go!

This beautiful little daily art journal will keep you creatively fired up! I hope you find this daily art journal practice to be a helpful and fun addition to your creative journey.

Christy Kale is an Austin-based creative entrepreneur, painter, mosaic artist, photographer and writer. As the CEO and founder of Christy Kale Fine Art, she creates artwork channeling Joy, Beauty, Light, Flow and Love, enabling her audience and collectors to live more joyful and inspired lives.

https://www.christykaleprints.com

https://www.facebook.com/christykalefineart

* * *

64

Anonymous Art Brings Smiles to the Heart by Marlis Walker

D o you enjoy making others smile? How about bringing a smile to others anonymously? I promise this is fun! Follow these easy steps to bring a smile to others, and to yourself as well, and there are no skills required!

Let's make brightly-colored birdhouses to hang around your neighborhood or city... anonymously!

Supplies you will need: A small bird house with a jute cord or small rope, etc., on top for hanging (Dollar Tree, or Amazon have inexpensive ones or maybe you know someone that can make them for you. Score!) You will need 2 to 4 paint colors, two inexpensive paint brushes (¼ to ½ inch will work depending on the size of your project. I suggest a flat and an angled brush to help paint the tight places)

Remember to paint the bottom of your birdhouse. Those birdies fly all around so you want them to see bright colors from all angles! You will want to use some sort of waterproof sealer to seal your paint on the birdhouse. Polyacrylic will work and you will need a separate brush for this. Do this step outside. (Follow the directions on the product of choice) If you are sharing this project with those youngins, I suggest an adult do this step. (Kids Love This Project Too!) You can make these as simple or elaborate as you want! You may even want to glue laser cut wood hearts, stars, or letters to your beautiful birdhouse! The sky's the limit! Are you ready?

Gather those supplies and start painting! You'll be smiling and laughing all the way through this project! Just think about all those people you will be making smile when they find them! I can't wait to see you, your projects and where you hang them! Please send pics to my FB page below so that I may share in your joy! Let's make this a movement! #ShareTheJoy

My heart is already smiling! Always remember:

Dare to be you.

You are one-of-a-kind.

And you are never too old or too young to try something that makes your heart smile. Others will be glad you did!

Marlis Walker of "Dare To Be You Designs By Marlis" is a self-taught, late-blooming artist (she started painting on canvas at the age of 60) who inspires, encourages, and teaches others to find their creative joy so they can "color outside

the lines" in every aspect of their lives while bringing joy and smiles to themselves and others. Marlis says, "Find that creative spark that makes your heart smile and share it with others."

https://www.facebook.com/DareToBeYouDesignsByMarlis

* * *

65

Ancient Mind Protocol for the New Economy by Kamila Behrens

Time to Implement: Starts to work on Day 1 and changes everything when practiced with consistency over time.

What You'll need: Ability to learn, 15 minutes daily

Overview: Today we are living with a wealth gap not seen since the empires of old, levels of unemployment that used to start revolutions, total electronic surveillance and erosion of privacy, an environmental crisis, technology and softwares performing many jobs, a global economy built on fraudulent banking and continuous war, and many more new and chaotic things that make it difficult to thrive.

Traditional ways of thinking like "go to college and get a good job" are essentially worthless. This crazy world calls for a growth hacking mindset, skillset and toolset. Human design and lifestyle businesses are the new "normal."

When we work with clients privately we teach hundreds of growth hacks in all of these areas but today we will share the most foundational and ancient one of all, growth hacking yourself.

All the good things will show up when you get on this path.

Step-By-Step Process:
Step 1: Sit down each day in front of a wall.
Step 2: Look at the wall in mindfulness for 15 minutes.
Step 3: Breathe in and out.
Step 4: Do Nothing. Just be in the moment.
Step 5: Repeat DAILY!

Conclusion: Once you are able to allow and be with less reactivity—congratulations.

This is when you hacked the mind and ALL things are possible.

There are many tactics and business practices that we teach to our students, from creating bestselling books to starting companies, but nothing beats synchronicity and awareness. We've seen this change thousands of people, and create incredible "unbelievable" successes for them in all areas of life. This cannot actually be explained; it has to be experienced, so make sure to stick with the DAILY aspect of this growth hack. Feel free to take it up to 45 minutes a day over time.

Kamila Behrens was born in the mountains of Czechoslovakia when the country was a Communist regime and came to America for freedom. After many adventures in many places, Kamila is now an author, mystic, philanthropist, serial entrepreneur and spiritual teacher with students from all over the world. She graduated university with the highest possible honors in Philosophy and holds a Dr. Div. Her non-profit institute is focused on common sense solutions to community development. Her consulting company is focused on helping movement leaders and subject matter experts write books and create income with their teachings, then invest the income into real estate, nonprofits and other permanent passive income assets.

https://www.behrensandcompany.com/clb

* * *

66

Conclusion

About the Author

*Jessica Hughes is a visibility expert for creative entrepreneurs as well as an internationally collected fine artist, #1 bestselling author, and mom of seven. She is founder of **Jess Hughes Media** and **Illuminated Press**, a boutique publishing company created to amplify the voices of thought leaders, artists, creatives, educators, and experts.*

*She is the visionary behind **The Creative Lifebook**. Her passion is supporting the audience growth of hidden gem entrepreneurs so they can step into the spotlight, lead with confidence, and illuminate our world. She offers educational programs, courses, and coaching to support value driven leaders with their mission to create true impact in the world. She teaches the mindset, skillset, and inspired action to be unstoppable.*

Hughes has been a featured expert on ABC, NBC, FOX, TED, Forbes, Chopra, and more.

Interested in contributing to The Creative Lifebook Series? We want to spread YOUR single creativity hack/tip/strategy to the world so everyone can benefit from your guidance to live a more creative life. Send an email to hello@creativelifebook.com.

You can connect with me on:

- http://www.creativelifebook.com
- http://www.facebook.com/jessicahughesfineart
- http://www.instagram.com/jessicahughesfineart.com
- http://www.jesshughesmedia.com

Subscribe to my newsletter:

- http://www.creativelifebook.com/hello